BECOMING A
WEALTHY
WOMAN
ON PURPOSE

YOUR GUIDE TO CREATING WEALTH
CONFIDENTLY AND UNAPOLOGETICALLY

HADRIANA LEO

To Zizi and Xen.

You help me do brave things

TABLE OF CONTENTS

PREFACE

Dear Reader,

I am so excited that you have chosen to read this guide. I am also humbled because, I have never written a book before. I mean, I have published articles and poems but never a whole book and certainly not one on personal finance.

You choosing *this* book is most affirming and I thank you for making that choice.

I wanted to write Becoming a Wealthy Woman on Purpose because I was constantly being overtaken by the overwhelming need for what I share in the pages. I keep meeting women who are not being served in the personal finance space and they feel helpless to do anything about it.

These women are crying out for someone to see them and acknowledge that the status quo was not meeting their need. They are trying to muscle through their financial circumstances and burning out. They are giving up on their dreams because they see no hope of bringing them to life.

If that is you then this book is for you!

You will find in the pages to follow a system for exploring your wealth and developing your unique formula for success. As you implement the action items you will discover amazing things about yourself. Your strength and resilience, creativity, and unique gifts to offer your world.

Most books on personal finance are admittedly boring but not this one. I was certain to write in the tone of my work with clients. You will find gentle truths and firm support. There is no judgement of your present or past circumstances. Your past money mistakes are not used to shame you but to highlight how you have managed to carry in despite them. Whatever you have done with your money in the past, this book is a soft place to land and from which to launch confidently into extraordinary living.

This guide is bursting with great information and still easy to read and the concepts shared are relatable and speak to the real struggles and triumphs women like you are facing.

Having said that, the content is not necessarily easy. It will challenge you in ways you may not anticipate. Stay open to it and trust the process. Trust in the dreams you once had that you have let go.

The ideas I share here have been revolutionary in my own life and have had significant impact in the lives of the women and families I have been blessed to work with.

As you read, I want you to feel supported. You are not alone. Know that there are other women just like you who are taking brave steps to change their lives through their finances. Feel their collective energies cheering you on and holding space for your success.

I may not be able to work with you one on one, but this book is a good starting point to healing your financial wounds and moving to that next level of wealth.

It is my absolute pleasure to bring this work to you. I wish you abundance, wellness, and wholeness.

Only the Best,

Hadriana

INTRODUCTION:
IS THIS THE PATH FOR YOU?

There are tons of templates, guides, and courses out there that help you manage your money, invest, and save. There are also countless resources that help you explore your money mindset and the roots of your money behaviour. So why this one? Why should you read *Becoming a Wealthy Woman on Purpose*?

This approach is not for everyone. It is not an approach that everyone needs or even wants. It requires you to go deep because the desired results are extraordinary and life changing.

And no, there is no magic formula. There is no Rule of 72 or a unique way to read the markets to ensure your success. Sometimes I wish there were, but where would be the fun in that? What I *have* discovered is a proven system of approaching wealth and purpose that will create your unique, extraordinary experience with money.

You can make this system your own and as such you will go inward to create the right environment that produces the desired outward results.

I will admit that I am proud of the results that I have been able to get for myself, and my clients by doing this. I celebrate the women who have taken the lead in their families and reached out for help to understand their money. I stand with the women who decided that the life they're living was unsatisfactory and therefore unacceptable. I am ecstatic about the massive amount of debt that we have been able to eliminate all while living lives of joy, freedom, and abundance.

Everyone, even those who identify as men, can benefit in whole or in part from exploring this approach to wealth. However, when you consider the investment of time, the nuances of this approach and the internal work that is called for, there are four characteristics that describe the woman who would be the most aligned with and have the most success with this system.

- You are in command of your finances, working hard, making good money but the numbers are not working. You've worked your way up the income ladder but until now you have been moving your numbers around to create budgets but they're not working.

  Every time you mess up with your money you have rejigged your budget, saved more, or spent less. Yet something keeps tripping you up. The numbers all add up on paper, but in practice they don't work out.

  If that is you, then this approach to wealth is for you. It will work for you in identifying the missing elements that you may have not considered. Those elements that exist beyond the numbers.

- Your numbers are working, but you feel like something's missing. You have started to realize that the healthy savings and more than enough spending money

2

are not giving you the feelings you thought they would. That raise at work from your promotion was great at first but now it is not sitting well with you. You are now able to take that vacation or buy that bigger house but you're just not getting all the awesome feels you were expecting.

This approach is for you because you are realizing that the life you desire and deserve is made up of more than just the money that you would accumulate. Now you just need to know what to do next. You are ready to explore the more meaningful nuances of your wealth.

- You need more support than a spreadsheet or template provides. Apart from loving or hating spreadsheets, you need a way to customize your wealth experience. You want to be confident in your ability to make changes and adjust as you move forward.

This approach is for you because you are empowered to take your wealth into your own hands rather than remain dependent your entire life on someone else to know what's best for you financially.

- You know deep, deep down that there is more out there for you. With every fiber of your being, you know that there is more for you to be and do, and you are ready to explore it. Your current reality is not your destiny. And, you know that what is in store for you is epic.

This approach to wealth is the one for you because it takes you through the varying stages of wealth from meeting your needs to creating impact and change as you fulfil your purpose. This approach is for you if you know that your reasons for creating wealth might start in your heart and mind but have a massive positive ripple effect on the world around you—well beyond your line of sight.

Prepare to challenge what you thought you knew about wealth. Open yourself up to thinking beyond a bank balance. Get ready to push your boundaries and create an extraordinary life. In the pages that follow I will share with you stories of women who did just that. While their names will be changed to protect their identities, their struggles and triumphs are real.

Becoming a Wealthy Woman on Purpose was written to address the needs that we women have which are not being met in the world of financial services. It is also beautiful in that it incorporates every aspect of who you are and superimposes that onto your wealth journey. This approach is fulfilling and wholesome, not greedy and tacky.

It is important to state here that this approach to wealth is not anti-male in any way. It is not anti-marriage or anti-partnership. This is not a radical feminist manifesto where women take over the financial world.

Becoming a Wealthy Woman on Purpose is simply a guide to help you develop the confidence, strategies, and support systems that you need to create the life you dream of—with or without a male partner.

This is a good time to assess where you are on your personal wealth journey. This will help you establish a starting point for your exploration of this guide. If you haven't already, take my quick online Stages of Wealth assessment at https://moneynavigator.ca/tools. The results will indicate where you are now, what challenges you may be facing, and the best actions to take in order to make it to that next level of success.

Throughout the guide, I have provided opportunities for you to process the information that I share. Journal prompts at the end of each chapter will give you questions to think through that will help you apply the concepts you just learned. Feel free to use the space provided to record your thoughts.

So, let's dive right in. Here's to you confidently and unapologetically creating wealth!

JOURNAL PROMPTS

How would you describe your current stage of wealth? What do
you enjoy? What would you like to change?

_____

_____

_____

_____

_____

_____

_____

_____

_____

_____

_____

_____

_____

_____

_____

_____

_____

_____

_____

_____

_____

_____

_____

_____

_____

_____

_____

_____

_____

_____

_____

BECOMING A WEALTHY WOMAN ON PURPOSE - WHAT DOES IT MEAN?

You may be asking the question, what exactly is a Wealthy Woman on Purpose and how can you become one?

First, I will tell you that in coming up with this description I was talking to women, serving them, listening to what they needed. Becoming a wealthy woman on purpose came to life in my mind as a double entendre, a term or phrase that could have dual meanings.

In this instance, becoming a wealthy woman on purpose is deliberate in its duality. It is deliberate in looking at two sides of a coin because for so long, when it comes to women and wealth, it's been "my way or the highway" of the male dominated finance space. You either do it this way or prepare to not be considered, to not be served.

The first meaning is this: if you are a woman and you want to build wealth, it will have to be deliberate. It must be intentional. So, becoming a wealthy woman on purpose means that you are going to deliberately, intentionally, and on purpose, take the action steps that help you become a wealthy woman.

Let's break that down a little bit.

Wealth building is no accident. Anyone who has acquired any degree of legacy and impact creating wealth did so deliberately.

So, let's say that, even with the odds so steeply against you, you win the lottery. You would probably be thinking, "Finally, I am wealthy now". But are you really? Perhaps you can get a big bonus at work, or you are the top salesperson, or the highest achiever in your commission-based job and get big money. Sweet, right? Sure! But *making* money is one thing. Creating wealth is another. Earning mind-boggling commissions is fantastic but creating multiple income streams is true stability.

Now don't get me wrong. I love a touch of serendipity as much as the next person but that can't be the basis of my wealth strategy or yours. Get after it and leave nothing to chance. Specific, strategic actions are the building blocks of wealth creation.

The second meaning, and perhaps the meaning that is dearest to my heart, is this: using your wealth to achieve your purpose. You see, for women especially, becoming wealthy is often very tightly woven with being on a mission of purpose—your purpose.

This definition of using your wealth to achieve your purpose is where a lot of the power lies. This is where you get the numbers to be worth the commitment it will take for you to create that wealthy life. By going deeper, you can find that place where both your head and your heart agree.

Before going further, let's acknowledge that the world of financial services was not created with you in mind. Just by facing the world as a woman, you are at a disadvantage when it comes to creating wealth. But knowing what you're up against is no reason not to proceed. That is the very reason you need to go a little bit deeper and a little bit further by becoming a wealthy woman who is "on purpose."

I acknowledge that when I refer to women I am painting in broad strokes. But if you face the world as female and the world sees you as female, they box you in and say, "Sit over there. This is how you are going to experience money." That prescribed experience may be at odds with how *you* want to interact with money.

As women, we are often driven by different things than our male counterparts. We are moved to action by different criteria and metrics.

Consider that not many men think of money through the lens of violence against women. Well, I can tell you that money, the access to it, the ability to use it, is one of the deadliest weapons used to keep women in abusive relationships. Of course, the issue of abuse is much broader than that. But when financial oppression is a key ingredient to controlling women, it becomes imperative that women have the opportunity to build confidence and financial competence so they can make brave choices for themselves and their families.

You see, becoming a wealthy woman on purpose is acknowledging that,

1. You have a purpose. You have a unique reason for being where you are, for doing what you are doing and for occupying this space you currently do in the world. And what happens is, once you can tap into that purpose, your success with money is certain. Because our drivers are powerful.

11

For example, a family may decide to maximize their education savings contribution for their daughter. For the male contributor, he may be driven by the thought of accessing all the free grant money the government will add to their plan. For the woman, she too wants access to grant money, but she is driven by the desire to give her little girl every educational advantage and opportunity she can to help her thrive. She, mom, knows all too well what it will take for her daughter to be seen, heard, and respected in an often-cruel world.

Knowing your reason for implementing a plan will fuel the actions you need to take because you are passionately committed to doing them.

2. Vision is magnetic. Michael Beckwith is credited with this quote that I love, "Pain pushes until vision pulls". I relate it to my decision to work out and take care of my body. I counselled myself not to wait for the doctor to say, "get healthy or die" for me to pursue a healthier way of life. Being so averse to workouts and balanced meals was forgotten once I adopted a vision of my healthy life. The same can happen for your finances.

Your mortgage agent may not understand how you were able to save such a large down payment in such a short time, but you know. You saw your aging parents and your growing children that both needed you present. Your vision of a home large enough to comfortably house all the important people in your life in one space made it easy to save that money.

You get to decide how you want to experience wealth and how you want to interact with money. Do you want the pain of shame, anxiety, stress? The pain of saying no to your children for things that you really would have wanted to give them? Do you want that pain to be what moves you to change?

Or do you want a vision? A vision of a life full of impact. Full of opportunities. Of freedom to do and to be.

Which do you prefer to be the thing that moves you? I invite you to choose vision. And the beauty about being a wealthy woman who is focused on purpose is that you get to do it your way!

While we all face the world in similar ways and have similar experiences, everything about our walk on this planet is unique. And the purpose that you have been placed here to achieve, no one else is going to do it.

That means that you need to become a wealthy woman on purpose your way. Your wealth journey will be unique to you. Do not try to adapt to a system that was never created for you.

Instead, create a system that is going to benefit and celebrate you—a system that embraces everything good and beautiful and challenging and purposeful and delightful about you. Understand the rules of the game, and then play to win.

Take for example Liz. She came to see me when she was having trouble making her large monthly mortgage payment. It wasn't that she wasn't earning enough. It was just such a struggle to have that lump sum available on the withdrawal date. She just couldn't seem to keep the money around for long enough. She decided to make weekly payments to her mortgage which totaled her monthly payment amount. Great solution, right? Not so much which she discovered when she got a delinquency notice.

I was able to share with her the rules of the mortgage payment game. Her weekly payments were considered extra! And while she was making all these weekly payments the bank was still looking for their large lump sum mortgage payment each month. She was deflated learning this, but we had a solution.

Instead of dealing with the bank and changing the terms of her mortgage, we simply created a separate account where she would pay her mortgage out of. Now, instead of making weekly deposits to the mortgage, she would make them to this new account. In doing so she removed the mortgage payments from her main activity account and was certain that the money would be available when it was time for the monthly payment. She created a system that celebrated how she wanted to manage her money but also met the requirements of her mortgage contract. She learned the rules and played to win!

Becoming wealthy on purpose provides many benefits.

1. It gives you permission to create the life that you want, the life that you deserve. Not by anyone else's standards but by the standards that allow you to live your best life.

2. It gives you permission and the opportunity to fund change. I don't know how many times I listen to people who say, oh, I just want enough money to get by. Nonsense. You know what? Let me tell it like it is. The change you want to see takes money. Don't sit at home and complain about all the things society should be doing. Add some funding to that feeling of dissatisfaction and suddenly, you get seen and heard. Fund the creation of new and healthy ways of doing and

being. Fund the change you want to see instead of sitting there complaining and doing nothing about it. Oprah Winfrey's Leadership Academy for Girls is a great example of how you can use your money to create change. She identified a challenge. Looked into where and how she could make a difference and she did it.

3. It gives you permission to eliminate distractions. I find a lot of times, women who have wealth and no purpose attached to it are the ones that typically make the entertainment news or the "wow, did you see that!" Women with purposeless money are the ones that are the biggest distractions, and they give wealth a bad name. On the flip side, the women in the world who use wealth purposefully, typically do not make the news. The Kardashians' latest family drama drowns out Melinda Gates' daily work in providing contraception to poor women around the world. And the Real Housewives get a steady viewership while the world may never hear about the work of Olajumoke Adenowo who is using her wealth and influence to mentor women and girls into becoming transformational leaders. They are quietly creating massive change and having a significant impact in their chosen fields because they are driven by purpose. No distractions, they just shut out the noise because they are working their wealth.

4. And finally, it gives you permission to create wealth. And why do you need permission to create wealth? Because as a woman, we are often told that wealth is not for us, it is not the thing that we should be going after. The messaging is that we should be sacrificing to take

15

care of everyone else, putting ourselves behind so that others could shine. Incorporating purpose into your wealth journey gives you the freedom to create wealth confidently and without apology.

So, let's celebrate your journey to becoming a wealthy woman on purpose. Permission granted.

JOURNAL PROMPTS

What does purpose mean to you? Have you identified your purpose? How could purpose bring more meaning to your wealth journey? What is one thing you can do that could help make your money decisions more purpose-driven?

_____

_____

_____

_____

_____

_____

_____

_____

_____

_____

_____

_____

ARE YOU A
WEALTHY WOMAN?

Answering this question can be complex. You probably defaulted to a quick calculation of how much money is in your bank account right now. Is your answer an automatic 'heck, no?' Your thinking may be based on someone else's definition of what a wealthy woman should look like or could look like.

Not too long ago the world was saturated with the phrase "alternative facts". If you're like me you probably thought, how could there be alternative facts? If it is a fact, it is a fact. There can't be an alternative. Let me suggest that, in answering the question, "Are you a wealthy woman?", there may actually be room for alternative facts. I say this because what has traditionally been given to us as facts, are actually someone else's opinions. In the world of wealth, many things that were touted as factual were merely opinions right from the get-go.

We have been fed other people's systems and because we don't fit into those systems, we are told that we don't meet the supposed standard. What I want you to consider here is this. It is possible that wealth can be individually defined. And, not just individually defined but also accepted as a correct definition regardless of how different it may be from someone else's.

When you define wealth, it allows you to take your own journey. So, with this in mind, would your answer be different? Are you a wealthy woman?

To help you develop your wealth definition, let's take a look at how wealth was defined when it emerged in society.

According to Merriam-Webster, the word wealth is derived from "weal", a long obsolete term which means "a sound, healthy or prosperous state; wellbeing." Wealth had a contextual meaning that had more to do with being well and less to do with money. Unfortunately, since its first use in the 13th century, wealth has become more about dollar signs and zeroes preceding the decimal point.

I love the original definition. It provides room for wealth to encompass all of you. That does not eliminate the numbers, but it broadens the definition to relate to the whole person being well.

In truth, money touches all aspects of our lives. It is a universal currency that is used to exchange value. Once upon a time, you could have exchanged two cows for building materials. Or paid for your doctor's visit in ounces of gold nuggets. That is not the case in modern society. The establishment of money as the standard for exchanging value means that the more money you have, the more you can acquire. That has sadly become the limitation placed on defining wealth.

To help you determine a true answer to whether or not you are a wealthy woman, I am going to share with you two things to stop doing and two to start doing.

1. Stop running away from big things because you are afraid. You may be facing hurdles to wealth and legacy

creation that make them seem so far away and out of reach. One of the ways your mind protects you is by lowering your expectations. You tell yourself that you only want to have a roof over your head. That as long as you're healthy, you will be fulfilled, and all will be well. That thinking comes from a misunderstanding of your purpose.

It is born out of fear and is designed to spare you from disappointment. It's true that when you set big goals and fall short it hurts. But I want to encourage you. Answer, "Yes, I'm a wealthy woman," not because you've settled for the safe life but because you've embraced the fullest, best, and highest manifestation of your big dreams.

2. Stop letting the system define wealth for you. So, let us be clear, I have established this before and I am going to say it again. The system that birthed financial services and personal finance as we know it, was not designed with a woman in mind. Therefore, we cannot expect to thrive and maneuver within a system not created for us and let that same system define our sense of wealth. That's not a winning formula.

3. Start embracing every aspect of wealth. All the money in the world cannot restore physical or mental health. And the pursuit of monetary abundance should never come at the cost of your spiritual, mental, or physical wellbeing. When you take a full-person approach to wealth you invest in being whole not just being rich. No part of you gets left behind.

4. Start claiming your wealth! I don't know about you, but I am so tired of having to go to "the man" for support. You have this great idea but have to trot it out to all these uninspired money men in the hopes that one of them will consider you worthy. I am so tired of it.

We, as women, are nurturers. We have great plans and grand ideas. We have great initiatives that we want to get off the ground. We can see it. We feel it but often, we can't fund it.

Well, it is time for us to go get the money. Don't let yourself be stuck in a position where you are stalled in your purpose, in your dreams, in your impact on the world, because you don't have access to the money you need.

Your wealth is out there. The longer you sit without your purpose-driven wealth, the longer you let other people dictate your life.

Even now, I am thinking of women, both in my personal and professional relationships, who feel like it is too late. They feel like they have reached a point where wealth is not for them anymore. They're tapping out before their round is done. True wealth, when properly defined, is there for you and it is yours to reach out and claim, even now.

I believe that you have access to wealth that is designed specifically to fuel your purpose. All you need to do is get off your nice little seat, your throne, whatever it is that you are sitting on that's super cushiony and uber comfortable and get *un*comfortable. Get out there and go get your chunk of wealth because the world is waiting for your impact.

Take the example of Cindy, a well-respected business owner. Before she claimed her purpose, she played it small with her business. Satisfied with having a few clients here and there and getting by. Then something amazing happened. She explored and claimed her raison d'etre and found a no-compromise reason to become, not just an entrepreneur but a CEO. She didn't only restructure her business for massive success, but she also created a program that provided loans for other female business owners to help them grow their businesses while feeling seen and understood.

So, are you a wealthy woman? I would love for you to answer honestly. And for that answer to be a purpose driven, holistic and brave "YES!"

JOURNAL PROMPTS

In answering "Are you a wealthy woman" consider these questions.

What areas of your life are creating positive impact? Do you have the financial means to create the impact you desire to make? Are you well? Operating at your best mentally, spiritually, physically, and emotionally?

_____

_____

_____

_____

_____

_____

_____

_____

_____

_____

_____

_____

_____

_____

_____

_____

_____

_____

_____

_____

_____

_____

_____

_____

_____

_____

_____

_____

_____

_____

_____

HOW DO YOU BECOME THAT
WEALTHY WOMAN ON PURPOSE?

For a long time, we assumed that if we just bought the right stocks or we saved the right amount of money, we would become women who made money and were independently wealthy.

Thankfully, and perhaps sadly as well, we have realized that we cannot save our way to wealth. We have also had to acknowledge that as women there are systems working counter to our objectives that prove difficult to counteract.

So, how exactly do you become that wealthy woman on purpose? Over the next few chapters I am going to peel back the process and break it down for you.

What you will learn is not found on Google. Neither will you hear the Dave Ramseys of the world sharing this. All the gurus out there that are asking you to cut your lattes and cancel your subscription to Audible, cancel cable and all of that, they are not speaking the whole truth. Retraction, repression and lack is not how you become that wealthy woman on purpose. The truth is that only by opening up, exploring and expanding will you realize your abundance goals.

My unique approach is encapsulated within the C|A|R|E methodology which I have developed from the experiences of the women I have had the privilege to serve. C|A|R|E turned out to be the perfect acronym because it not only encapsulates a method that works but it also communicates the fact that women need to connect with wealth in a way that exudes genuine care for themselves, their families, and their communities.

Before we proceed let me share with you a conversation I had with a beautiful young lady. She shared that she was so looking forward to becoming her best self. Earlier in the conversation, she had shared how she was finding it so difficult to stay on top of her money and make "sensible" money decision on a day-to-day basis. Almost her entire view of herself and her relationship with money was negative, distressingly so.

Now, back to her "best self" comment. I had to stop her right there. I had to share with her that, in this very moment, she was already her best self because every moment that we have, every experience, every challenge, every choice that brought us to this moment are all part and parcel of us being our best selves. So, at this moment, you are your best self.

Similarly, please know that you are already a wealthy woman on purpose in this very moment. The question then is will you decide to walk in agreement and alignment with that truth? Will you decide to bring that truth into a physical manifestation where you create the results of wealth and purpose?

That is where confidence, strategy and implementation come in. That beautiful combination of elements, purposely put together will manifest that person. It will bring that dream to life and the world will see that indeed you are a Wealthy Woman on Purpose.

The C|A|R|E methodology incorporates four key elements. We will explore these in depth in the chapters to come. For now, here is a brief introduction.

Clarity.

Clarity is a word that gets bandied around a lot, especially in entrepreneurial circles. And while I hate to be another user of a cliché, it is imperative that you view your journey to wealth with clear lenses. The lens through which you see yourself and the lens through which you see the world must be unfiltered and unobstructed—clear on your goals and your dreams. That kind of clarity in wealth is going to revolutionize your money – how you earn it, spend it, relate to it…everything!

Now the clarity I speak of is not about standing in front of the mirror and repeating affirmations. Affirmations can be a tool, a resource to be used in your journey to wealth but so can meditation, journaling, and prayer. Each of those are tools to aid your journey, not a be-all-end-all. Becoming a Wealthy Woman on Purpose begins with clarity. Get super clear.

Alignment.

In this step you will explore balance and fit. The beauty that exists here is that when you have come to a place of clarity, the work of alignment is smooth and fulfilling.

What often happens in the world of personal finance, we look for alignment primarily based on how much a strategy can grow our money. Or sometimes we give priority to copying what other millionaires are doing. We want our lives to be like this person's and to have that thing.

Alignment requires that you peel back many, many layers to understand what wealth needs to look and feel like for you. It must also create balance in other areas of your life as well. You cannot have balance in one area and not have balance in another.

Results.

So many of the women that I have been blessed to work with are tied to a strategy. Even if it is not working, they are committed. They are holding on until the end come what may. Well, we're not doing that here, ladies. Instead of grinding your way with no results, learn to critically review what's happening with your journeys to wealth, with the realization of our dreams, and demand results. If results are not coming, let go of the strategy. Define the results you are expecting.

Not just *what* results, but also *when*. Are you expecting your defined results today? Should it come a year from now? Or is this one of those things that will deliver to another generation, well after you have passed on? What results are you going after? Additionally, how are your results going to be measured?

It is important to realize that dollar figures are not the only metrics that will be used to measure your results. We will explore results from the perspectives of wellbeing, wellness, and wholeness. Remember, there's more to wealth than dollars.

Evolution.

I always think it funny that, me, a firm believer in creation, one who believes that the world came to be intentionally and not by accident, should be a proponent of evolution in any part of life. Let me explain.

I believe that with deliberate attention to our clarity, alignment, and results, we have the opportunity to evolve into legacy creators, freedom fighters, and impactful women on this planet. Changemakers and nurturers that have access to the resources needed to create the world we want to see. We don't have to be begging, setting up Go Fund Me's or sitting quietly in a corner hoping to be approved. We get to evolve and become. I love the word become, and I love everything that it stands for, everything that it inspires in me because in my mind, becoming is a journey. It does not happen at the snap of a finger. It is a journey of a lifetime.

Let me assure you that even as you are going through this journey, at every stage you will be living a life that is full and rich, meaningful, and impactful regardless of what part of the C|A|R|E process you are working through.

So, why C|A|R|E? Because it has been missing. In my market research, I see one segment of people who just focus on the mindset. They do these affirmations, heal their money wounds, deal with the traumas, and eliminate money blocks. I see all of that, and it is great work. I do it too.

On the other side, I see those who just work the numbers. Let's set up a spreadsheet, put some numbers in and do whatever it takes to fit your life into those numbers.

31

They say, invest $600 every month for 30 years, you are going to be a millionaire. Or invest in houses and rent them out, or the stock market and that is your surefire way to wealth. That is the length and breadth of the strategy, and it is the only way, as far as some are concerned.

What C|A|R|E does is bring together a merger of the tools women need to create wealth. Confident clarity, aligned strategy, results driven implementation and impactful evolution. A full spectrum approach to wealth that resonates with the needs of women and offers them the gift of wealth on their terms, without apology.

When you add C|A|R|E to your personal finance you will reclaim your confidence, your contributions to the world, and your wealth. Becoming a wealthy woman on purpose may not happen overnight, but standing in that truth now, the truth that you already are a wealthy woman on purpose, is a game-changer, dare I say, a life changer.

JOURNAL PROMPTS

What areas of the C|A|R|E methodology do you think you need to focus the most on? Where do you feel strong?

_____

_____

_____

_____

_____

_____

_____

_____

_____

_____

_____

_____

_____

CLARITY

GAINING CLARITY
FOR WEALTH BUILDING

One of the biggest struggles my clients mention when we start our work together is overwhelm. They are often overwhelmed by everything that they must learn, or do, or be part of. The overwhelm is real.

I know in my case, whenever I am overwhelmed, I stall. I get paralyzed and can't take that next step or do that next thing. These are the times when there are a hundred and one things to do but you will find me curled up under the blankets eating Cheetos and losing myself in fiction.

I have found that the biggest contribution to overwhelm is lack or loss of clarity. And as it relates to wealth, overwhelm occurs when you lose sight of why you're doing the thing you're doing. It could also happen when what you're doing is no longer meaningful to you.

The actions you take to create wealth should be grounded in a vibrant clarity about what you want out of the wealth-building experience. In addition, you should be clear about what you bring to the experience, what you want from it, and where you want it to take you. Clarity in wealth-building is essential and multifaceted.

I have been wearing glasses since I was a teenager. I still remember the first time I sat with the optometrist. He brought this huge machine to my face, and I had to line up my eyes with the openings. I could hear these clicks and spins that sounded like gears shifting, spinning, and turning. That first time was a bit scary, but I have since come to understand and appreciate the process.

The optometrist had to first figure out why my vision was blurry (click, spin, turn). He worked his way through a series of adjustments (more clicking, spinning, and turning) to find the best solution for me. He clicked, spun, and turned his way to providing me with clear vision. That experience, from my first to my most recent pair of prescription lenses, created a customized clarity solution for me. And, as I grew older, as my body and technology changed, my prescription for clarity changed. That could not have been achieved using a templated ten question survey with multiple choice responses.

Every single visit to have your vision checked is a custom visit. Layer upon layer, the lenses are adjusted, and the result is analyzed. All with the ultimate objective of you experiencing your clearest vision possible. That's the kind of process that forms the foundation of your clarity in wealth. It incorporates examining and adjusting several different components of your experiences with money.

Imagine waking up in the middle of the night for a quick bathroom visit. This time, though, you are not in your own bed. The layout of the room is foreign to you and there is very little light available.

If you try to find your way in the dark you will be hesitant, slow, unsure because you can't see well enough to make quick progress. Depending on how vivid your imagination is, you may even start seeing monsters in the shadows and end up embarrassing or even hurting yourself trying to get away from them.

Your lack of clarity in this scenario is costing you time, undermining your confidence, and putting you in a negative emotional state. The same thing happens when you try to manage your finances from a dark, blurry place.

But what if you found the light switch?

Now, you'd be able to trade your slow, hesitant steps for confident strides. You could be nimble in anticipating and avoiding obstacles. And when you operate from a positive emotional state you could face your monsters and see them for what they really are – challenges to be met.

What a difference clarity makes!

You will create your clearest vision by first examining the different segments of your wealth vision.

As each of these components gets refined, they get clearer, they get better optimized and your vision gets crisper, sharper. That is when you are truly ready to create wealth.

Let me introduce the four lenses that we will be adjusting to gain true clarity for wealth building.

First, the emotional lens. Emotions are not traditionally a consideration when dealing with money. In fact, more often than not, we are taught to keep the emotions out. And when working through the Results section of this C|A|R|E process, I will counsel you to keep the emotions out. But here, when you are seeking clarity, you MUST consider the emotional lens through which you view and experience money.

Now this is not about turning money into a cry fest. Sure, cry if you must but it is not a requirement. What you must do is take an honest look at the emotions involved with you and your money.

Every single day you are making unconscious decisions that relate to your money and your wealth. How do I know this?

Harvard professor Gerald Zaltman, in his book How Customers Think: Essential Insights into the Mind of the Market, reveals that 95% of purchasing decisions are subconscious. Further, I like how noted neurologist Richard Restak puts it. He said, "We are not thinking machines. We are feeling machines who think."

This research supports the prevailing theory that we use our emotions when making spending decisions and then use logic to justify our actions. So just imagine. With every swipe of your card, you are seeking an emotional response before questioning the cost of your purchase. That explains why so many of us know logically what we should be doing with our money but find ourselves doing something else.

It makes sense, then, that you should become well-acquainted and crystal clear about the emotional components of our wealth journey. When you get clear about how your emotions are contributing to your financial actions, you can then make better decisions about your wealth.

Next, you need to adjust your mental lens. I cannot tell you how many times women say to me that they are not good at math, have never been good at math, and are not interested in getting good at math. And I sit there and think, what does math have to do with it?!

Think back to all the complex formulas you had to memorize in high school. Don't look at me for any help. I tapped out at calculus. How much of this turned out to be useful in your daily, personal life experiences? For most of us the intersection of math & money can be summed up in addition and subtraction operations. Maybe a percentage calculation here and there and most of us have mastered those concepts. Am I wrong?

Instead of thinking that you need to be good at math, consider that the mental muscles you need to build are in the areas of resiliency, stick-to-it-iveness, and determination. That is the kind of mental work you're going to have to do because the road to wealth is not a straight line.

I was born and raised on the beautiful island of St. Lucia. It is a small, mountainous island with many a winding road, literally. I remember as a teenager climbing Gros Pitons, one of our world heritage sites. Not the highest mountain on the island, but one that can be climbed by the average fit person.

Well, when I climbed it back then, I was kind of dating this guy and the adventure had little to do with the trek and everything to do with the guy! I remembered next to nothing about the climb. So, a few years ago, on one of our visits home, I thought, let's do it again, this time with the same guy, now my husband, and our two teenage daughters.

Well, let me tell you the girls almost disowned us. The climb was not what they considered a vacation experience, but we made it to the top and came back down again. I was glad that I did it again because it allowed me to experience the trek anew and learn some lessons about how you ascend to the top of mountains, and wealth.

What I learned:

- Straight lines to the top can be treacherous. Gros Piton has a twin peak – Petit Piton. Climbing to the top of this beauty is only attempted by professional mountain climbers. Why? Because it is a steep, sheer climb. Climbing Gros Piton reminded me that it is often better and safer to wind your way up at a manageable pace while never losing sight of the goal.

  Steep climbs in wealth are not sustainable and should only be attempted by sophisticated, professional wealth builders who have the tools and support systems in place to manage the endurance required to make it to the goal.

- Sometimes, as you're climbing you may need to go down a bit. Along the path to the summit there were many times we went downhill for a bit before climbing again. The same happens with your journey to wealth. Don't be afraid of dips or taking steps back. They provide opportunities and paths that will make your journey safer, more pleasant, and more achievable.

- The steps aren't neat and uniform. From one step to the next, you could be crawling on all fours to get on top of boulders or stepping confidently on solid wooden planks. Knowing that the next step could call on me to be flexible was an exercise in expecting the unexpected.

With your wealth journey, you must prepare yourself to be nimble. Sometimes you will need to take baby steps and crawl along as you learn. Other times, you will need to trust yourself and the journey, and leap ahead. Either way, stay the course to the top. Your vision fulfilled is there waiting for you.

- You have a better time at the top when you enjoy the journey getting there. Stop and rest when you need it, take in the view here and there, take some selfies with silly faces along the way.

  In your journey to wealth, don't get so fixated with the end that you forget to live in the present and take in all the beautiful aspects of your journey as you go along.

All these lessons point us back to the need to adjust how we think about and experience our journey to wealth. It's not about math but resiliency. About not taking no for an answer. About being so committed to your end result that you are willing to take a step back in order to launch forward. Your mental capacity to make decisions and to stand and advocate for yourself. Your ability to not be beat down by the system but instead to work that system to your advantage.

Adjust your mental lens as it relates to money so you can create the experience you want to have in wealth.

The third lens that needs adjusting is how you view your present situation. Many women experience wealth in one or another extreme. Either things are horrible, or they are perfect. And what makes it worse is that they also often personalize these experiences. So now it isn't the experience that is horrible or perfect but themselves. The sad truth is that an unclear view of your current situation is often the result of you internalizing how others see you. You have so long bought into judging yourself by how others are living their lives and what they are sharing about their own experiences.

All those picture-perfect selfies on sunny beaches mean nothing. The big house with the fancy car in the driveway actually says very little about the financial situation of the owner. But that's not what we have been sold.

Getting a true understanding of your present situation requires that you dust off the distractions of other people's lives. You are to remove the influence of the Joneses and focus on your own goals and dreams. Perhaps, you've been lying to yourself for too long and you need to remove the rose-coloured glasses and see things as they truly are.

It's like driving in the downtown core when you have to depend on a GPS. At certain points, when the skyscrapers obscure the signal, directions are useless because the system cannot properly determine where you are. As long as your current position is inaccurate, the directions will make no sense at all. In the same way, being clear about where you are now is imperative to determining how to get you to where you want to go.

Now don't get me wrong. It isn't always the case that your situation is worse than you think it is.

I had a call with a young lady who shared with me that she had money left over at the end of the month and how horrible she felt because, obviously she was doing something wrong. She beat herself up so much because she knew she should be doing something with that money instead of having it just sitting in a chequing account. First off, I shared that this was a problem that many women wished they had. Then I helped her see that what she was viewing as a problem was actually an opportunity! She should be excited about what could come out of this "problem".

We created a plan that gave every penny a job to do. She took that large chequing account balance and invested a chunk of it with a professional advisor for long term gains.

Next, she identified some short-term goals she wanted to achieve. Some went to her vacations. Every other year she would take an epic adventure. In between those years, she planned for girls' weekends and road trips.

Now her chequing account takes care of her day to day needs and her money is strategically deployed to help her realize her goals and dreams.

She could stop beating herself up and live a life that was meaningful and felt like her truth.

Isn't that so often the case for us women? We beat ourselves up no matter where we are on the wealth spectrum. Sometimes the clarity we need is to see how well we are doing and to better acknowledge the opportunities that are available to us.

So, it's time to bring clarity and truth to your present situation, the good, the bad and the costly. Acknowledge what is working well and what isn't. Get real with yourself so you can bring to life your extraordinary dreams.

Finally, the fourth lens to get clear with is your future. I'll be honest with you. My future lens was almost completely blacked out. It was hard to see through that lens because I had stopped dreaming, and I had let the system and circumstances obscure my dreams. I was afraid to keep dreaming.

When it came to money, my expectations, and the legacy I wanted to create, I looked no further than the next day, the next bill, and the next paycheque. I avoided thinking about wealth altogether because I had written off that possibility for myself. As a result, I was going nowhere, and fast.

I knew two things. I was unhappy with my present circumstance and the vision of the future was dark and depressing.

As I gained clarity about my future, MY future, I grew more hopeful. As I got brave enough to make that vision my own, to lean into the desires of my heart and the impact I felt compelled to make on the world, things started changing and new life and clarity came to my expectations of the future.

None of this clarity exploration is easy but this part, in particular, can be a struggle. This is where you must take a chance on yourself and the power of your purpose. This is where you have to buy into a future that is so compelling yet, at this point, sits just outside your reach. This future vision may even seem impossible. And yet, with clarity, it pulls you forward.

In chasing clarity for your future, you will challenge all the societal rhetoric that constantly bombards you, trying to dictate what your life should be. You will uncover a strength like you've never known to dream your own dreams, chart your own path, and build wealth that fulfils your purpose.

I invite you to clear off that future vision lens to uncover a life that is not only possible, but highly probable as well.

These four lenses: your present, your future, your emotional, and your mental lenses, are the four key components that you need to ensure you maintain sharp focus to become that wealthy woman you know you can be. Let's break down how to explore clarity in healthy ways.

JOURNAL PROMPTS

Do your actions bring you closer or take you further away from the vision you have for your life? Is your financial situation really as bad as you've been thinking, or can you cut yourself some slack? How do you relate to money? What are some of your triggers that generate negative results?

_____

_____

_____

_____

_____

_____

_____

_____

_____

_____

_____

_____

CLEARING YOUR HEAD AND HEART FOR WEALTH BUILDING

The emotional and logical aspects of wealth are sometimes portrayed as fighting against one another. As I shared before, we make decisions emotionally and use logic to justify them after the fact. Well, I want to offer you an alternative. One where emotion and logic, head and heart, work together, complementing each other and creating a harmonious result for your wealth experience.

Clearing your head and heart takes care of the first two lenses, the emotional and mental areas of your financial life. But I don't want you to think in terms of your competency to manage money or emotions. You are competent. That's not up for debate. We all are competent and have access to all the resources we need to manage money well.

The head and heart experience encompasses the exploration of your gifts and your saboteurs. The tricky bit here is that your gift can easily become your saboteur or vice versa.

A great example of this is a common condition many women face, that of analysis paralysis. It is generally viewed as something that holds you back, keeps you from doing what you want to do, or achieving what you want to achieve. At its root, analysis paralysis is the result of your head and heart working counter to each other.

If you suffer from analysis paralysis you are searching for answers, hence the analysis. When you're not finding the answers you want this creates stress and anxiety, hence the paralysis.

But consider this. Analysis paralysis is usually experienced by people whose gift is analysis and who operate best in environments where they can control or anticipate the outcome. They are trying to use that gift to guide their next step forward.

But when you look at analysis paralysis through the emotional lens, you'll see that it is actually a protection mechanism. It happens when you want to avoid disappointment and failure. You've probably been taught, by society or personal experience, to distrust your emotions, distrust your gut instinct.

The real challenge here is not the need for more analysis. It is the need for confidence to take the next step. Now because analysis is considered to be your gift, you go there for confidence. But it won't be found until you can correctly instruct your emotions and expectations. That instruction comes in understanding that you won't always succeed. That failure is always going to be a possibility. That you might just miss something. And that all of the above is okay.

Analysis paralysis is a confidence issue and a good example of how your gifts could be your saboteur when head and heart are disconnected.

The fix? Connect your head and heart with clarity. Understand the limitations of your gifts and the freedom that exists in your perceived weaknesses. Until you can do that you will remain in analysis paralysis or life might force you out of it and that is never a good thing.

While you're sitting there waiting for a sure thing, opportunity keeps passing you by. You need to get your head clear, and you need to get your heart clear. Your gifts must operate to your advantage and allow room for your emotional needs to be considered and met.

As a woman on her journey to wealth, give your emotions their rightful place. Clarify those emotional responses. Understand where they are coming from. Instruct them to either affirm their accuracy or understand their role in protecting you. Either way, your emotions cannot and should not be overlooked.

Getting clear in head and heart identifies your strengths and then asks how you can use them to create the emotional response you desire from a specific aspect of your wealth journey. It also acknowledges that there are limits to what your gifts can do. That there are times when you must lead with your gut and rest in the rightness of that decision.

I worked with a realtor once who was finally gaining traction in the business and netting six figure annual commissions. She could not understand why, for the life of her, she couldn't find two pennies to rub together although she was making what many would consider big money. It seemed to her that the more money she made, the faster it disappeared.

Now she had tried many things. The budget spreadsheets, money management apps, the affirmations in the mirror and more. Nothing was working. So, we stopped and peeled back a few layers of how she related to money and where she learned her money lessons from. What we found had no logical roots, but they were there all the same.

Somewhere in her upbringing she had created a belief that people who are wealthy either get sick or die. This came from her experiences as a child in her community. As she grew up her heart and mind found experiences that reinforced that belief and it stuck. So, guess what? Her conscious actions were the result of the unconscious desire to live as instructed by her childhood experiences.

She was allowing money to leak from all kinds of holes in her financial behaviour. Her head said she should build wealth, so she worked hard to earn money. Her heart said money will bring sickness and death, so she worked hard to get rid of it. You might think to yourself, that's not logical and it makes no sense to you but that's the power of the unclear connection between head and heart.

So, once we can get clear about the roots of that belief, where it came from, and how it was impacting her decision-making she was able to find freedom to earn, save, and build wealth so she was not in conflict. She was now free to make progress in her wealth journey.

As you seek clarity in head and heart things will come up for you over time. You will continue to discover interesting contributors to your actions and beliefs that you can either celebrate or decide to root out. The important thing is that you are seeking clarity. I am still discovering things, uncovering trauma that contributes to my money stories.

Come with me again to my island home of St. Lucia. This time I will introduce you to my parents. Or perhaps I should say my experience of my parents since what I will share has never been discussed and reflects only my own interpretations and observations.

These two amazing humans built their lives out of nothing and sacrificed so much to change the trajectory of their lives and that of their children. They worked multiple jobs, did manual labour, and were looked down on by others in "higher" society. They did this with staunch determination because they wanted us to have the opportunities that they didn't. They wanted us to have the advantages in life that they weren't given. I know this now but growing up I didn't have that perspective. By the time I was born, the last of many children, their sacrifices had started paying off.

My observations at that time were full of conflicting money stories. I saw my family managing two nice houses while many of my neighbours could barely keep a small structure over their heads. We had two vehicles, one for my dad and one for the kids, while many had none at all. I thought we were rich.

What I heard, however, was something different. I heard a lot about making supplies "stretch" and finding the cheapest running shoes for school and the rising cost of school supplies. I also heard what was not said. The distrust of wealthy people and the idea that what we had wouldn't last. That frugality was virtuous and enjoying life too much was irresponsible.

Needless to say, I was confused and without active dialog about our circumstances, I made up my own stories. In retrospect, I could see that while the external circumstances improved greatly for my parents, the deep scars of lack remained.

I deal with these conflicting ideas about money with most spending decisions I make. Here's how I resolve this conflict between what head wants and what my heart is feeling.

I remind myself to choose ease and abundance for myself. My parents' trauma is not mine, so I deliberately release claim to it. Some days I can do this exercise all in my head. Other times I need to journal and pray through it.

My head and my heart can agree once I see clearly that I can make different choices without conflict. I can still love, honour, and respect my parents while making different choices with my money. I can choose to spend for fun not just for sustenance.

Now that you understand that the head and heart work together in your wealth journey, you can seek opportunities to adjust your perspective and challenge your viewpoint.

A good place to start is whenever you find yourself doing that thing that you know you should not be doing. That is the first and biggest indication that you have some unconscious emotional contributors to your behaviour.

It's like our struggle with fitness and nutrition. When we beat ourselves up for not taking that walk or showing up for the workout. Or when we wolf down that second extra piece of delicious dessert knowing full well that it will result in an uncomfortable bloated experience a few minutes later. Why do we do it when we know better? Because the action is satisfying an emotional response that we have yet to acknowledge or instruct.

With the awareness that you have gained in this chapter, do the brave thing. Challenge, examine, instruct, and reset any blurry or unfocused viewpoints that exist between your head and heart. Challenge your perspectives. Are your beliefs around money serving you or holding you back? Do your actions bring your vision into sharper focus or blur it further? Every time you choose to fine-tune the head and heart connection, you have an opportunity to reset them to a place of clarity.

JOURNAL PROMPTS

Can you think of a time when your head and heart did not agree in a financial decision? How did you resolve it? What could you have done differently? Do you find that you lead with your head or your heart first?

_____

_____

_____

_____

_____

_____

_____

_____

_____

_____

_____

_____

_____

CLARITY IN THE PRESENT ENSURES YOUR FUTURE WEALTH VISION

B ut what about the past, you're asking? Well, clarity about the past is tricky business. Early on in my coaching practice, I spent a lot of time diving into the past with clients, looking at the decisions they made with money, how they interacted with money, what were the contributors to the choices that they made, and so on. As you can imagine, everyone has a story. Here's what I learned.

Delving into past money behaviour is like stepping into quicksand. It gets sticky and becomes so hard to move on from because you keep finding new stories and retelling them with "if only I had…" That is not beneficial to clients at all. So, I've adjusted the approach.

Hindsight is 20/20 so there is no need to work on gaining clarity there with two exceptions. In the process of becoming a wealthy woman on purpose, we visit the past only for the purposes of celebration and/or forgiveness.

We do this because the question *why* can become a black hole when we look back at our money decisions. We tend to forget the full scope of circumstances that surrounded the decisions we made.

I remember using my home equity to buy a car. At the time, I thought it was a great decision because I would not have a car payment, I still had lots of equity in the house, and I was able to finally buy the car I wanted instead of the one with the payments I could afford. An all-around great decision. Fast forward a few years when we got into real estate investing in a bigger way and here I was beating myself up because I could have used that money to buy an appreciating asset instead of a car that has since depreciated a great deal.

I could have sat in that space of *why* and regret, and remained stuck with unresolved emotions. Instead, I made the decision that I recommend to you now. I celebrated all that I got out of making that decision (a nice car, comfortable driving experience, etc.) and moved on to developing a new strategy to create the opportunities I wanted in real estate.

You cannot change the past so please do not get stuck in it. Celebrate the positive and forgive yourself for the negative outcomes that came about as a result. If you find yourself repeating negative behaviours, then revisit clarity exercises for head and heart to find the root cause. Now pack up your past money mistakes and get moving on because there is a present and future that needs your attention!

A clear understanding of your current financial situation is the setup for a future with goals and dreams realized. This clarity goes beyond what is happening on the surface. It requires more than just assessing whether or not you have enough money to pay the bills or if the kids can go to their favorite camp this summer.

It is so easy to see the symptoms because they are exhibited on the surface, but dig a little deeper to identify the root cause.

Enter Mary Jane. She reached out to me to help her get a handle on her debt because she just couldn't seem to manage it. She was making extra payments with every paycheque and still not making any headway in lowering her debt load. In fact, if anything, things were getting worse.

The symptom – increasing debt. Her remedy – make more debt payments. On the surface that seems like a great thing to do, so, why was it not working?

Mary Jane was treating the symptom of a deeper problem. She was not earning enough money! You see, no matter how much she cut back on expenses, her income was just not enough for the life she was currently living. Let's me break if down for you.

In a month, Mary Jane was bringing home about $3000 and cumulatively making about $2000 in debt payments. Now with rent being $1500, that's already half of her take home pay and she hasn't eaten yet! Before she got off the start line, she was already behind.

Her frustration came from not having a clear understanding of her present situation. Every so often she would look at her chequing account and see there was money sitting there so Mary Jane would make a payment towards her debt. In her mind she saw extra money but was there really extra? Certainly not. So, what inevitably happened was, when the time came to shop for her groceries, put gas in the car, buy a dress and take care of her phone and cable, she would end up using, you guessed it, her credit card. And with the vicious cycle that is revolving credit, she kept accumulating debt instead of eliminating it.

Because Mary Jane was unclear about her present situation, what she thought was extra money was actually money for which the payment date had not yet been reached. What she thought was a debt problem was a symptom of the fact that she was not earning enough to live on. She was never going to cut back enough to make this work.

That is why clarity about the roots of your current situation is so important. You may be giving your best shot at fixing the wrong problem.

Clarity in your present allows you to choose the right strategy and approach to bringing true relief to whatever your money challenge might be.

Now imagine you're Mary Jane. What is your internal dialog in this situation? This sets up the perfect environment for all the "I'm not good with money", and "I can't get this right," and What is wrong with me?" and so on. The imposter has found the "evidence" to support the false narratives and you and money become even more estranged.

So, get clear about your challenges as well as your successes and opportunities. Because when you get clear on your present, you can create a solid foundation to confidently create your future.

So, let's talk about that future for a bit. Getting clear on your future requires that you do some scary hoping, dreaming, expecting. It requires that you get out of your way, take a chance on what's possible and decide to make it real for you. I encourage my clients to live their future today. Here's what that looks like.

First, describe what you want your future to be like. Express that picture in sensory terms, how your future looks, sounds, smells, feels, even tastes.

Then, take some quiet time to immerse yourself in that experience. During your meditation or prayer time, go to that future place. Be in the moment with the experience. Feel all the feels.

Finally, when your sensory visualization is complete, bring all those emotions back with you into the present. The objective is for you to live that experience every day. It is for you to be so intimately familiar with the future you are creating that you can conjure it at the snap of a finger.

One big roadblock to success with gaining clarity of the future is that we often tie our future to other people's wellness or success. What do I mean? It is easy to define your financial future from the perspective of your children being well or your charity of choice being well-funded. Your future is viewed through the lens of your life partner being beside you and your bosses being kind.

I challenge you to view your future from your perspective looking out. From the place where you are well and can benefit others, and not from the place where your future depends on the actions and outcomes of others.

That perspective must also be based on what YOU want. Not what you should want or are expected to have or be like at a certain age or time in your life. What is your future?

Once you have absolute clarity on what your desired future will be, you can then extrapolate that vision outwards to see how others would be impacted.

I guarantee you this. If your future vision is first about others and not about you, it will not have the power it needs to carry you to its fulfilment. Instead, it will wear you out, drain and deplete you.

Clarity in your present and future is essential. The bridge that will connect your present financial situation with your future wealth vision is that daily sensory experience. That state of mind, state of being that infuses your future vision is what will make achieving your goals worth doing and non-negotiable.

With wealth being a state of mind, you can engage that state effortlessly when your vision of the future is clear. Adopt a wealthy state of mind by living in your future daily.

JOURNAL PROMPTS

What areas of your financial life are you unclear about? How could that impact your future goals? Is not realizing your future goals an acceptable outcome for you? What would happen, how would you feel if your goals were realized?

_____

_____

_____

_____

_____

_____

_____

_____

_____

_____

_____

_____

_____

ALIGNMENT

ALIGNMENT
FOR YOUR WEALTH!

My first thought when I hear the word alignment is the wheels on a car. Whether or not wheels and tires are your first thought, I think you can relate to something in your life that was out of alignment, whether physically or otherwise. I am sure you can call to mind some experience with alignment or the lack of it.

And yet we do not think about alignment in terms of wealth. Why is that? We've already talked about the systems and programming that go into why you think and relate to money the way you do, so I won't revisit it here. I will, however, say that, especially as a woman, you must make the exploration of alignment a key part of your journey to wealth. Lack of alignment is what prevents you from connecting the dots in personal finance. It is why for some money just does not make sense and is so unrelatable.

Personally, alignment was a big part of me taking ownership for my dreams becoming a reality. I was a licensed financial professional before starting on this journey so, if anyone understood money it was me. But understanding money and owning my money-funded dreams are not the same thing.

Standing in the truth of my purpose, vision, and best life required that I go on a diligent search for alignment. This exercise did not require seclusion, or a special manifestation or meditation session. It was by no means a woo-woo type of experience at all. It was, however, a season of hard questions. Of challenging if my thoughts were really mine. A season of scary revelations that taught me so much about myself and my expectations.

Alignment was the catalyst to me venturing into real estate, investing in a meaningful way. Making money in real estate was and still is a big part of why I wanted to become an investor. However, the money alone was not worth what I perceived to be the headaches and risks that I knew would be part of the experience.

To make it worse, I was exposed to events and successful investors who were being measured by how many doors (think units or properties) they had or how much their portfolio was worth. None of that resonated with me but I knew that this was a tried-and-true wealth-building avenue.

So, I had to look for alignment. Once I was able to find it, I had no problem participating in real estate investing and the strategies that I chose for myself were a great fit. I had no resistance. There was nothing keeping me back. There was nothing holding me from actually taking the next step and then the next, and then the next.

Here are some of the things you may be experiencing as a result of financial misalignment.

A rough ride

Have you ever been in a vehicle when the wheels are out of alignment? I have. The worse the misalignment the worse the ride. Same thing for your wealth journey. A rough money ride that has nothing to do with the markets or your seasons of wealth can only be rectified through repairing your financial alignment.

Financially speaking, misalignment shows up when you are using products, techniques, or strategies that you don't or cannot relate to. You want to push forward but you are uncomfortable, sometimes embarrassingly so, by what you think you should know but don't. What you don't understand but hesitate to ask. That feeling of being the only one in the room who doesn't get it.

It is that kind of misalignment that has you up all night. At three o'clock in the morning when the rest of the world is sleeping and the person next to you is snoring, you are tossing and turning and cannot turn it off. That is the rough ride of a misaligned wealth strategy.

Yes, there will be challenges, and yes, you will have setbacks. That is par for the course. But what most women suffer with is misalignment. The good news? We can fix that!

Abnormal Wear and Tear

Another thing that can happen when you are out of alignment is you get disproportionately worn down. Things that excite others just tire you out. You have no lasting power for any one strategy or plan. Before long you are ready to walk away from it all and revert to the comfort of your lackluster financial existence.

I used to workout at a CrossFit gym. I loved it. I remember my husband commenting that this was the only workout program that I had stuck to for so long. I still love these workouts. The thrill and challenge. The camaraderie and support. Functional movements with either high reps or heavy weights. It was really the best fitness experience I've ever had but I no longer do them.

One of my nemesis movements was box jumps where you would jump off the floor and plant your feet onto a box, a stable, raised surface where you would then plant your feet, stand up straight and then jump off. A workout could easily require that you do this over one hundred times, sometimes in conjunction with other movements, for a great challenge and a beneficial workout.

Well, I remember so clearly the day I got my CrossFit rite-of-passage bruise to my shins when my feet jammed on the side of the box and my shins took the hit. Boy did that sting. I still have the scar. But I digress.

I am telling you this because, as much as I love CrossFit, the traditional programming was out of alignment with what my poor knees could take. While I was all hyped up during the workout with the happy juices flowing, I was fine. But fast forward to heading home and climbing or descending stairs and girl, I hurt and it only got worse as the day went on.

The thing is I was using a method that was painful and making an existing problem worse. My knees were being worn down at an alarming rate and when I finally went to have the joints imaged, I had osteoarthritis and I wasn't even 40. I was building beautiful muscle, toning up nicely, but my knees! CrossFit did not cause my knee problem but it surely exacerbated it. I had to find a workout experience that took my current situation into consideration and could still deliver the outcome that I wanted.

The same thing for you. Misalignment causes you to be worn down, no matter how committed you are to the plan. Sometimes you are going to find some parts of your experience are just getting beat up. You experience anxiety, stress, and discomfort that's more than just growing pains or a learning curve.

Lack of Progress

Significant misalignment causes your financial progress to be extremely slow or even non-existent. If it is really bad, it will literally break you or, when working with couples, it will break your relationship.

It is so frustrating doing all this work, putting in all this effort, doing all of the worksheets, attending all the webinars, learning all the jargon and all that jazz, only to find that you are not making progress. It's one reason I hate treadmills. Hustle and grind and go nowhere!

The forward momentum you are struggling to generate and not succeeding at is a symptom of your misalignment. Either your strategy, timing, implementation, or support systems need realigning.

Affirmations are not working? Misalignment. Faking it and still not making it? Misalignment. Lots of talk and no action?

Misalignment. Busy doing and not getting anywhere? Misalignment.

Read on to discover what causes misalignment, how to fix any misalignment that may exist, and why you really should prioritize making alignment a mandatory and regular exercise in your wealth journey.

JOURNAL PROMPTS

What areas of your current financial situation feel off? Which techniques, tools, or strategies have you implemented but are unsure about? What would you like to change about these techniques, tools, or strategies?

_____

_____

_____

_____

_____

_____

_____

_____

_____

_____

_____

_____

RECOGNIZING
WEALTH ALIGNMENT

I have found that we so often focus on what is wrong and not working that we miss everything that is right in our money experience. As a result, we don't get to celebrate our wins because we don't even realize that we're winning.

I like to say that if it walks like a duck and quacks like a duck, it must be a duck. A well-aligned financial duck. Well, not so fast. We know that this isn't always true because there are imitations out there that fool you, make you think it is a duck, but it is no duck. That's especially true in finances where keeping up with the Joneses is the way to be (even though many protest vehemently that they're not doing that). The result is having the look of wealth on the outside while being woefully miserable on the inside.

So, how do you recognize when you are wealth-aligned? How do you know when you're in a flow with your money and dreams? I like relating wealth alignment to the seasons.

I did not experience the seasons of a temperate climate until I was in my twenties when I came to Canada as an immigrant. It was quite interesting as an adult to experience my first snow. Although I'd seen it on TV, it's nothing like actually living the experience of snow and freezing cold on a clear, sunshiny day. I have derived many life lessons, many sources of encouragement and wonder from observing the seasons change.

In your wealth journey you will go through seasons. It won't always be your favorite season. And your favorite season won't always be someone else's. But you can accept that there are seasons and appreciate (or at least tolerate) the cycle of change.

The same is true for your wealth journey. There will be times to harvest the fruit of your labour and times to go inward to replenish energies and resources.

Wealth alignment is finding peace and flow with the seasons of wealth. It is trusting the processes and plans that you are implementing regardless of the stage you are at.

Now, I want to be clear that being at peace with where you are does not mean that you are going to stay there. Settling is not part of alignment. And I will share more about that when we get to the "E" in the C|A|R|E methodology – Evolution. The peace of alignment comes from forgiveness of your past, contentment in your present, and anticipation for your future. Financial alignment brings peace in knowing that as you do your part, the Divine will take care of the rest.

Another sign of alignment in your wealth is preparation and adaptability. You understand that a lot of things in your wealth journey are experiments. You are trying something to see how it works, what the result is, and what you can tweak. How does that sit with me? Where does this not sit right?

Some women say that they don't want to be a real estate investor because they don't want to be a landlord. Fine. But there are so many ways you could participate in real estate as an investor and never be a landlord. So where is the problem? Where is the misalignment? Can misalignment be a product of misinformation?

Yes, absolutely. So being open and nimble enough to learn and adapt is essential. It's like moving your bum in a chair until you find that sweet spot that is both comfort and support. Sometimes you've just got to throw the chair away, let's be honest. Sometimes there is no comfortable position, especially in those bougie chairs that cost so much money but are hard as concrete.

Alignment prepares your mind and resources to adapt for your most efficient and best result. It does not change who you are to fit the journey. It adjusts the journey to suit the beautiful, wonderful you.

Wealth alignment brings you joy. A 100% return on all your investments would make you happy, even ecstatic in the moment but would that bring you joy? Why do you think there are so many people with healthy, well-performing investment portfolios who are just plain miserable with their lives?

It's because, instead of joy, their results often create resentment because of what it takes to create those returns. They often resent the money they make, the time it takes to make it, the sacrificing of core beliefs and the relationships that suffer as a result.

And what happens next, makes them even more resentful. They think that, if they could just get the next pay increase or hit that magic asset value, then they'd make the time, prioritize the relationship, or stand on their values and finally find peace, joy, and fulfilment. A catch-22 if ever I have seen one.

There is a way to generate impressive results and experience joy in the process. It is called financial alignment. Never, ever sacrifice your joy for money. Wealth won't bring you joy, and joy won't bring you wealth. But alignment allows you to find joy in your wealth.

Finally, alignment in your wealth journey is purposeful. When your money has a purpose, it does amazing things for you. When your wealth journey is aligned you are not just working for another mortgage payment or a pair of shoes. These are all well and good, but you are working for so much more than that. You are working for impact and purpose.

This is at the center of you becoming a wealthy woman on purpose. You are going to go after alignment in your wealth, because you are driven by your opportunity to impact a person, a cause, a country, whatever it is. You are driven to become a wealthy woman on purpose, because you are focused on that unique reason you are here and you're going after it.

Let me quickly ensure you realize that creating your ideal, curated lifestyle is all part of living your best life. Being driven by purpose doesn't mean you cannot experience the comforts of life if you so desire.

Too many of us were led to believe that we had to choose lifestyle or purpose and we couldn't have both. Wealth alignment shows up in purposeful living that does not restrict you to poverty or lack. The beauty of purposeful, aligned wealth is that you get to create what works for you.

Aligned wealth will look different on the outside but on the inside, it will always be peace, preparation (adaptability), joy, and purpose. The people in the world that are creating the biggest impact on the world with their wealth are the ones who took the time to align their wealth experience. You get to be one of those people now. How exciting is that?!

JOURNAL PROMPTS

Make a list of everything that is right for you now with your money. What aspects of your money experience are bringing you joy, peace, and flow?

_____

_____

_____

_____

_____

_____

_____

_____

_____

_____

_____

_____

_____

_____

_____

_____

_____

_____

_____

_____

_____

_____

_____

_____

_____

_____

_____

_____

_____

_____

_____

_____

_____

WEALTH MISALIGNMENT.
WHAT CAUSES IT?

There are many people who have money but remain thoroughly unfulfilled. That is the biggest symptom of misalignment in wealth. It is a clear indication that whatever they're doing in creating and using wealth is not quite what they thought it would be.

So, what causes wealth misalignment? Essentially misalignment occurs whenever there is a conflict between how you make your money and how you feel about that experience. The experience may involve a specific strategy or stream, a method or vehicle that you are using to make your money. Any time there is a conflict between how you create wealth and how you feel about the wealth creation process there will be misalignment.

You cannot out-earn wealth misalignment. The cure for that misalignment you are feeling is not going to come from making more money. You also cannot outspend wealth misalignment. You don't get to throw money at misalignment because money is not what is going to fix it. You cannot outrun misalignment. It follows you around like a shadow. You cannot out-earn it, outspend it, or outrun it.

So, let's get a clear understanding of the root causes of your financial misalignment. That is the key to addressing the issue and developing a solution for it. To do otherwise would be a waste of time, opportunities, and precious resources.

There are three core areas where we can typically look to identify wealth misalignments.

The first one would be in the foundations of your relationship with money. It is one of the reasons why all Money Navigator programs begin with understanding how you relate to money.

I remember having a moral conflict in my charitable giving experience. I have always been a good church girl and part of that experience meant that I felt mandated (a very deliberate choice of words here) to give a certain amount of my earnings to the work of the church.

Things came to a head when I started earning more. Not that it wasn't an issue before, but when the cheques got bigger and bigger my resentment got worse and worse. It was getting to the point where I was almost wishing I didn't make so much money so I would be able to give less without resentment.

The root of the problem was neither in my charitable giving nor my capacity to earn. It was in the misalignment that existed in *why* I was giving. It was in the feelings that came up because I was giving out of obligation as opposed to giving because I genuinely wanted to.

So, I looked at how others gave. I talked to financially challenged individuals and asked them how they found such joy in giving. I learned more about the organizations that I was contributing to. I stopped myself in the middle of making donations and assessed how I was feeling and why. Once I did the work to examine my relationship with charitable giving, a lot changed. I still believe in making donations through my church, charitable organizations, and to individuals in need. The difference now is that I only donate out of a genuine desire to create or influence change, not out of obligation. I give because I choose to.

The difference? Alignment allows me to earn and direct my money happily. I am not conflicted or resentful about my contributions to any charities because I am deliberately choosing to make them.

For you it may be your hesitation to charge what you should for your service offerings. That is a sign that you have a foundational belief that is in misalignment with what you know you should be doing. No coach, program, or strategy can fix this until you resolve the areas where your misalignment exists.

If there is any misalignment, if you have any feelings of conflict around how you are earning your money, no matter how much money you make, you are never going to feel contentment, fulfilment, or create the life that you desire and deserve from it. You might have the trappings on the outside. You might have the lifestyle that so many would work so hard to have, but on the inside, it will never do for you what you thought it could, or what you wanted it to do for you.

This second area where you can look for wealth misalignment is in your lifestyle. By lifestyle, I am referring to what shows up on the outside. The life experiences you expected to have once you had money. This is not necessarily about keeping up with the Joneses. It is more about having what you thought you would once you had a certain level of wealth.

Is your money creating the lifestyle you thought it would? If it is not, you are in misalignment.

So, think about that power-broker executive woman. The one you look at and envy on the downlow until you find out that she resents the hell out of her job. And you think, if you had that much money you'd have nothing to complain about ever again in your whole, entire life.

What you don't see is a lifestyle misalignment that is being fought because that woman is earning a healthy, easy six or seven figures and resenting every bit of freedom, time, energy, or peace it takes from her. Why? Because she values freedom, time, or energy and thought that her money would get that for her. Instead, it is doing the opposite. It is taking too much from her that she values.

There is no strategy that is immune from this challenge. Real estate, cryptocurrency, stock market, you name it. If all you have is what you accumulate and you cannot create a life filled with what you value most, you are in misalignment.

In this kind of misalignment, your accumulated resources soon turn into headaches. You begin to hate having to do more or invest more or monitor more. You start hating what is required to keep all this up because you are not getting the feedback you need from all your efforts – the time to spend with family; the freedom to turn down nightmare clients; a good night's sleep; a house in the country where you're not tied to a desk.

Let me drop a little pin here to say that for every avenue available out there for building wealth, there are multiple ways to participate. So, if you are someone who wants to invest in the stock market, there are several ways you can do so and still maintain alignment.

Imagine that you are that person who wants to pursue an active real estate portfolio of rental properties, but you really value being flexible and spontaneous with your time. You do not want to have to drop everything when a tenant says that the toilet is backed up. You have some choices.

1. Become a property owner and give up your time in exchange for building that portfolio of rental properties. A look into my professional crystal ball shows that you won't be a happy landlord and will not last long as a rental property owner.

2. Choose to not become a rental property owner. You walk away from the entire idea because you are not willing to explore your options to make it work for you. You will nurture disappointment and that "if only" feeling of regret for a long time.

3. Become a rental property owner in partnership with someone who is not bothered by the time it takes to manage the day-to-day requirements. You share profits and responsibilities and both get to be hands-on in their areas of strength.

4. Become a rental property owner and contract out the day-to-day management to a company that specializes in that field. You never have to bother to find a tenant, repair a toilet, or fix a leaky roof. Someone is being paid to do it and you just write the cheque.

This is just one example where the source of misalignment was lifestyle-centered and can be resolved creatively.

Another more universal example is health. For every single human being, health is a vital requirement to enjoying your wealth. In fact, without health, wealth becomes useless and worthless.

You already sacrifice so much for others and it is easy to put your wellness on the back burner in order to pursue wealth. While you may not specifically identify health as something you value, it most certainly should be prioritized and protected at all costs. If you are pursuing wealth and your health is suffering, you are in misalignment.

You *can* do all the things and still prioritize what you value so you have the lifestyle and the results you want in your wealth journey.

Let's say that you have examined your relationship with money and created the lifestyle you want, but you are still unhappy, unfulfilled in your wealth journey. That is when you start to explore the third area where misalignment tends to stem from - impact.

There comes a time when every woman who is going to be wealthy on purpose will use her money to create an impact. This can happen at any stage of your wealth journey. So, it really is not about how much money you are making. It is about using your money to create a positive impact.

This misalignment shows up when you get that hollow feeling in conjunction with your money and you start thinking that you could be doing more. You start asking yourself if there isn't something more you can be doing to make a difference somewhere, somehow. You may even start thinking about what your money can do for you after you're no longer on this side of our human existence. When these questions start coming up,

90

it is time to look out for misalignment in your wealth that is stemming from your inability to create your desired impact.

As it relates to impact, we tend to relegate that idea to doing things on an epic, global scale. For most of us, that will not be the case, but we all seek impact. So even at your current level of wealth, you can be dealing with impact as a contributing cause of your misalignment. So don't exclude yourself from this exploration.

In fact, I would like you to consider that the lack of your desired impact could be a great incentive to get up and take that next step in your wealth journey. Lack of impact is a great reason to push yourself beyond just making enough. Enough to pay the bills, feed and clothe the kids, and so on. Your commitment to creating a positive impact is a great reason to create wealth.

Misalignment may happen over time. As we grow and change, the things that worked before may not work now. Your core values may not change but your priorities certainly do and will determine what gets your attention and when.

For example, when your hands are full raising babies, your biggest source of misalignment may come from lifestyle and not impact because you have a more immediate need for time flexibility as you earn, so you can show up for your children when they need you. You may still have misalignment in the areas of impact but that is not where you will focus first.

Or perhaps you are recovering from a divorce, and you are now challenged to maintain your desired lifestyle as a single woman. Your most pressing area of misalignment may lie in resolving your relationship with money in order to quash those old money mindsets. Lifestyle and impact misalignment may well exist, but they take a back seat to your need to be served as you deserve as a single woman building wealth.

We are all becoming who we are as time goes by. Areas of misalignment may change or become more or less urgent. That's okay. When you are struggling to keep your head above water financially, you are not in a place to be saving anyone else. Address your most pressing, most immediate areas of misalignment and as you heal and grow you will find more areas to refine your experiences with money and wealth.

There are times when your misalignment will resolve organically. As the circumstances around you change, your wealth journey may just right itself. Things will improve on their own and you will come to a place of fulfilment with your money. Your confidence grows, your support systems fall into place, and you become that confident, aligned wealth builder.

More often than not, your misalignment will require deliberate action to be resolved and to optimize your journey. Take the most direct path to your wealth so the benefits can be felt for as long as possible.

Misalignment can derail your wealth journey to the point where the best strategies in the world will fail you because you are not aligned. And you are more likely to fall for scams that promise you the impossible. I can promise you that the answers you must seek first are inside you. Lean into the divine that lives inside you.

The best way I have found to do this is to shut off external stimuli and look inward. First, set your intention to find the answer you are looking for. Then, through prayer or meditation open yourself up to receiving the answers you seek. I have found that the answers show up vividly in the quiet, intentional moments.

So, wherever you are finding that friction, wherever you are finding that rub in your wealth journey, in your wealth-building experience, I encourage you to take the time, dig down deep, find the cause of your misalignment, and right your wealth vehicle on that path to wealth. The path to the life you desire and deserve and the impact you want to make on the world. Because, as I like to say, when a woman has wealth in her hands not only does she change her world. She can change *the* world.

JOURNAL PROMPTS

Where do you currently feel the most misalignment: relationship with money, lifestyle, or impact? How is this misalignment showing up for you? What is something you can do to help create alignment?

_____

_____

_____

_____

_____

_____

_____

_____

_____

_____

_____

_____

THE FIX FOR WEALTH MISALIGNMENT

I have been out of alignment with my physical self for a long time. I shared previously my passion for working out and how, because I had not addressed some core issues, it actually made me worse off than before I began.

The kicker was that, instead of fixing the root of the misalignment, I just decided to push through it. I decided that I would place mind over matter. After all, I am the one in control of my body. My body will listen to me, and it did for a long time.

My body took all of the beatings I was giving it. I felt strong and powerful when I went through my workouts, but my body was out of alignment. So, guess what? I couldn't maintain it and I was not getting the results I was expecting. The experience was bittersweet, with more than a hint of frustration. As much as I loved my workouts, I was in such discomfort when they were done, I just couldn't keep it up. Ultimately I had to stop all workouts until I could repair the root causes of the issues I was facing.

When you are misaligned in your wealth journey the same thing happens and, in this chapter, I will share with you how you can repair the misalignment so you can get back on track to building wealth in a way that you love and that creates the results you want.

The good news is that repairing misalignment is easy. Misalignment happens when you are in conflict. When the various facets of yourself are not in harmony. So, the fix? Honesty. Yes. Honesty still is the best policy.

When you are being dishonest with other people, you feel bad. Your conscience won't let you sleep or look that other person in the eye. You can almost feel the fires of hell snapping at your heel.

But what happens when the person you are being dishonest with, the person you are lying to, is you?

One of my core values in everything I do is integrity. For me that means that I will only and always speak the truth in love. Imagine trying to build wealth, create freedom and impact while dealing with internal conflicts that threaten or challenge your core beliefs. This can happen when what you expect and what is expected of you are two different things.

In repairing the misalignment first identify where the conflict exists, and how you can deal with it in a way that is honest. In a way that is authentic. How do we address this conflict and repair misalignment in our wealth? Here are four areas to get honest about.

1. Be honest about your past.

The conflict that exists with your past money decisions shows up when you take the position of either victimhood or deliberate ignorance.

Ignorance because you put on your rose-coloured glasses and refuse to take an honest look at what contributed to you being where you are. You would prefer to not know. Channeling your inner toddler, you plug your ears, close your eyes, and sing as loudly as you can above the warnings that are all around you. And then when that does not work, when the signs around you just cannot be ignored, you move on to victimhood.

Victimhood because you choose to blame everyone and everything for your situation instead of looking at yourself. This victim mentality perpetuates a feeling of helplessness and the inevitability of lack. Victimhood places you at the mercy of your circumstances.

Instead own your results. Yes, there are circumstances that surround every money experience, but you need to stop that blame game. Step away from being the victim and take ownership of why you are where you are right now. Get honest with your past money decisions and actions. As stated before, resolve the past by celebrating the outcomes and forgiving the missteps.

Be honest about the driving forces behind the choices that you made that brought you here, whether the results are spectacular or not.

I heard this idea shared in a motivational audio track. Everyone is self-made. The world loves talking about self-made millionaires and celebrating them. We marvel at self-taught musicians. But we do not acknowledge the fact that many of us are self-made broke, self-made mediocre, self-made coward.

The life that you are living now is self-made. That space that you are in right now is an accumulation of decisions that you have made and beliefs that you have held that have landed you where you are right now. So, being honest about your past means that you stop playing the blame game and get real about why you are where you are.

2. Be honest about what you want

Maybe you want the bling. The comfort of not having to worry about money. The nice house, nice car, and the impact that money could create for you. Perhaps you want the stage. The recognition and affirmation that money could afford you. But you tell yourself you don't, or you shouldn't, want those things. As a result you live your life in a state of constant conflict.

Sometimes it's because these desires run contrary to what we have been brought up to want. Good girls are supposed to be quiet, unquestioning supporters of their husbands and find their fulfilment in serving others. We make ourselves small, bury our dreams, sabotage our purpose because of the misguided belief that our desires are somehow wrong.

Many women have chosen not to work with me because they are waiting for their husband. They are waiting for his support, his blessing to take the next step they know they must take. They are afraid of how the dynamics will be overturned if they take the lead. They don't want to rock the boat, but the family is suffering while they try to maintain the status quo.

Other times, the conflict exists because you don't believe in your ability to achieve these things, so you work hard to squash the desire. I mean, why wish for something when you have no confidence that you can achieve it. No one in your family or circle of influence has done it and, those women that you know of who have done it, seem to exist in another dimension.

It's like me and running. I have always avoided races, anything with a lot of cardio. I tell myself I am not very competitive. Speed is not my thing.

But there was the one time I was participating in a street party in my neighbourhood. For whatever reason I found myself setting up to run this women's race against my neighbours. I do not know how I ended up in that line because this girl doesn't run unless there's a dog running after me. But there I was.

Anyway, on your marks, get set, go! I am running, not expecting anything. But lo and behold, I found myself in second place. Well, let me tell you. This "I am not competitive" girl put some pep in her step. When I saw that there was an actual possibility of winning, I changed my tune… and won the race!

This is the experience of so many that I work with. Without the confidence that you can win, that your dreams could come true, you lie to yourself and say that you don't actually want the dream. You try to shield yourself from disappointment and end up intensifying the conflict. But should things change to create a high probability of your dream being realized, suddenly you want to win. You want the dream again. Don't squash the dream because you don't think you'll make it. Instead equip yourself with the tools and support you need to make the dream inevitable.

3. Be honest about how you want your wealth.

Why do I love Starbucks so much? After all, I am not a big coffee person, and I can't be bothered with the status symbol that Starbucks is for some people. So, what's the appeal? Me and millions of others love Starbucks because we get to make our beverage *exactly* the way we want it. We get to control the precise ratio of flavours that make that recipe uniquely ours. Your perfect mix might be too sweet or too bitter for someone else, but that blend is perfect for you. You even get your name on the cup because the drink is all you! Well, you should pursue the Starbucks experience for your wealth.

Be honest about how you want to experience your wealth. What is that unique blend of factors that would make this journey perfect for you? It might be different for your friends and may butt heads with the current industry wisdom.

While others are happy to get a cottage in the country as their second home, you can get busy working to build your second home on an island where the breezes are warm, the beaches carry that unmistakable scent of salt water, and time slows down.

Honesty requires that you know what you want, and you have determined your preferred criteria for achieving it.

4. Be honest about why you want wealth.

We are so stuck trying to be noble about why we want the things we do.

"I just want to have enough."

"I want to help my family."

"I'd like to help save the whales and end hunger."

"I only want my children to not have to face the same challenges I had."

Nothing wrong with these but do they represent the truth, the whole truth? Can we just speak honestly about why we want the things we do?

You can want something for the simple reason that you want it. There doesn't have to be an altruistic reason for everything we do. We don't have to save everyone before we give ourselves permission to just be. To have comforts, epic experiences, to want something for no other reason than you want it.

One of my goals is to have a house near the water. I love water. Water speaks to my soul. And a must have in my house near the water is a master suite retreat. A place where I can be cocooned away from everyone else... husband and children included. In this space, I am free to be and do whatever I want: reading a book, dancing to soca music, singing, whatever it is. I want that space where I can just be, without having to nurture anyone, lecture anyone, hug anyone, fix any boo-boos. And why do I want it? Because I need to be selfish like that sometimes. It is essential to how I restore my energies so I can go out and serve again. I need a space that is dedicated to pouring into me and not taking from me.

Society tells me that I should want a big house so I can comfortably host my family when they come to visit. The status quo says that I should probably not even want a big house. Imagine how that money could be used instead to help save the world. But I know why I want it and, in this knowing, comes honesty.

You only get to repair your wealth misalignment when you are honest. And until that happens, the misalignment will persist. It is up to you as a woman who has dreams to fulfill, that you make honesty your wealth priority.

The fix for your wealth misalignment starts with those eyes that are looking back at you in the mirror. Embrace the truth of your past money actions and beliefs. Then get real about what you want, how, and why you want it. Your wealth misalignment will begin to resolve, you will build aligned strategies for wealth and start seeing the results you are seeking.

JOURNAL PROMPTS

Where are you fudging, hiding, or straight out lying to yourself about your money? What are you scared to discover? How can you create an internal environment that will help you be honest about your finances?

_____

_____

_____

_____

_____

_____

_____

_____

_____

_____

_____

_____

_____

RESULTS

EXPERIENCING
THE RESULTS OF WEALTH

The confidence and strategy that you are looking for in your wealth journey are developed in the Clarity and Alignment stages of the C|A|R|E Methodology. With these in place, it's time to explore Results.

This is where you see the tangible manifestation of the clarity and alignment work you've done. And, because of the work you've done prior to this, your results will be fulfilling, long-lasting, and purposeful. The results you will explore here go so far beyond the dollars and cents of your investment portfolio. They are unique, amazing, far-reaching, and all-encompassing.

Early on when I started developing the Money Navigator programs, I would get looks from audiences when I'd say that you can be wealthy if you live in the projects. You can be wealthy even though you're not eating caviar or flying in private jets. As you maneuver through the various stages of wealth on purpose, your results will be different.

So yes, you can be wealthy while you are living in the projects and trying to maximize your income. You can be wealthy while improving your credit score and repairing that poor credit. Even while you are still just trying to keep to a decent cash flow plan. You can be wealthy in all these situations because wealth is a state of mind.

The results you are looking for are the ones that say you are doing the right thing, you are on the right track, you are making good decisions, you are getting good outcomes, you are improving, you are making better decisions than you did yesterday, you are consistent. All these are metrics that measure your progress. So, the amount of money accumulated and your net worth will not be the only measurements you use to determine your results.

No one else is you and your results may be entirely different from someone else's. That is okay. No one has that unique combination of vision, life experiences, and circumstances that are working both for and against you. Even when the results look the same on the outside, the why of the results may be different. So, as you are looking to experience wealth, as you are sitting in the results section of that journey, understand that someone else's results are not your benchmark.

You need to ensure two things as you explore your results. First, ensure that you identify your desired results. Then measure them.

Success can be measured in many ways. Take entrepreneurship, for example, a great wealth vehicle. How do you measure success in entrepreneurship? Depending on where you are in the business development process, success might not be measured in cash flow. Your business might be at the stage where it is focused on product development, testing, and research. Success may be a completed prototype or expansion into a new area. Revenue will always be a factor, but other metrics may be better indicators of success at various stages of your business.

The same for your journey to becoming wealthy on purpose. The external trappings are not a true measure of wealth and they definitely do not speak to a successful, vibrant, aligned wealth journey.

Tune into the results that you want. Think about the results that you would like to see manifested, created, and realized in your wealth journey.

Let's say you are earning well. Your credit is great, and you are good with spending and saving money. Making money is not your challenge right now. Instead, you might be challenged with finding ways to not have to work for every penny. So, at this point, your challenge is investing and having money work for you instead of you working for it. How can you measure your success in that space? What are the results that you want in this stage of your wealth journey?

Do you want to double your money in five years? Do you want to understand everything about a cryptocurrency so that you can become an informed, knowledgeable investor in that space? What do you want?

Next, once you know what you want, explore what living with those results would look like. In your mind, what would your life be like once you achieved your desired result?

I avoided wealth for a long time because I thought it was too complex. It was too complicated, too much of a headache, too much of everything I did not want. In my mind, an abundance of money would cost me my peace of mind.

Case in point, I did not want a big house because all I could think about was that I did not want to clean it. That is the only thing I focused on. The one thing that would complicate the dream.

Now, I choose instead to define not just the result I want but also how I wanted to interact with the results. I said that, yes, I want the house of my dreams. I also said that in order for that house to be what I wanted it to be, it must come with the capacity for me to also afford a regular cleaning service. I get to have the result and interact with it in a way that works for me.

In the next few pages we will explore how to create your desired results, make them stick, and get as close as you can to guaranteeing them.

JOURNAL PROMPTS

What do you want? And what does living with that look like? List all the ways you are already experiencing the results you desire from your money.

_____

_____

_____

_____

_____

_____

_____

_____

_____

_____

_____

_____

_____

TRACKING
YOUR WEALTH STATS

Wealth is more than a number, especially for women. In addition to the numbers, there are other metrics to look at. There are other things of value to you that you need to experience alongside the numbers. So how do you keep track of it all? How do you measure your progress?

First, let's be clear that whatever method you are going to use to track your results, it needs to be a method and within a platform that is easy for you to use. I love spreadsheets. I enjoy creating very intricate formulas that do all kinds of fancy things with numbers, charts, colours, and more. It's my thing but it may not be yours. You may have to rely on a different method of recording and tracking.

Good old pen and paper never failed anyone. I am a big proponent of keeping it simple. Not because you are not good with spreadsheets, but because you have better things to do with your time than to overly complicate something that should bring you joy.

Second, tracking your wealth stats should not be a depressing activity. It should be an expansive experience. It should give you lots of information and fuel you to take the next step. That does not mean that the results you are tracking are always going to be moving in the direction you want them to. That is unrealistic. There will always be curve balls. Tracking your results, however, should be an exercise in expansion, not contraction, learning not blaming, forward movement and not stagnation.

You should also know I am not the biggest proponent of budgets. It has more to do with the word and its connotation than the actual idea of tracking and planning your money. Language plays an important role in how we experience our lives and the same is true for our money. Be deliberate in using language that gives you the right feels.

Instead of budget, I use the term cash flow plan in all my programs. I think that it communicates more accurately the ebbs and flows of money around us and through us. Whatever words you decide to use, they should be meaningful to you and encourage your success. If you hate budgets you will resist working with them. Choose language that gives off the right vibes for you.

So, what should you be tracking?

Let's start with the obvious – your numbers. Do not be afraid to look at your numbers. For better or for worse, 'til death do you part, nurture an intimate relationship with your numbers and track them because they tell you all kinds of secrets.

I suppose it's natural to want things to happen fast. We want results, big results and we want them yesterday. Instead, set realistic as well as idealistic expectations. It is okay to have some goals that stretch you a bit. But also understand that where you are, you didn't get there overnight. And based on where you want to go, you may need to give yourself some grace to get there. So, set goals for your numbers and track those.

There is a plethora of apps that help you track your numbers. Some are affiliated with specific banks while others are independent and connect to your account. Either way, they help to pull and aggregate the information for you to help keep track of where your money is going.

Whatever you choose to use just commit to track your numbers in a way that allows you to be proactive. Don't only look at what you spent. Use that information to go forward and plan ahead for the next month or the next paycheck or whatever is going to be next for you.

The numbers that you focus on will depend on the stage you're at in your journey to wealth.

When you're independently wealthy and have everything you need, you might be tracking the return on investments of your stock portfolio because you want to ensure that the income you require is being generated without depleting your capital.

If you're the woman who is working an aggressive debt reduction plan, you will be tracking your debt load. You want to see those numbers go steadily down. You will track interest rates and revolving credit vs non-revolving to ensure that your amounts owing are steadily decreasing.

Maybe you used up all your retirement savings towards buying a house. Your focus is tracking your savings account. Prioritizing the rebuild of a healthy emergency fund and keeping to a healthy spending level to maximize your savings contributions.

A universal stat to track would be your income. Not only are women being paid a lot less than our male counterparts with equivalent training and equivalent positions, but we are also very hesitant to ask for a raise or to increase our prices as entrepreneurs. Keep a solid handle on your income and revenue streams, track those numbers because your income is what you are going to be using to create the life that you want.

If you find that your income levels have plateaued, you should proactively look for ways to increase your revenue. That may involve speaking up in that next performance review with your boss. You can share all the value that you brought to the table for the business and the contributions you have made to their bottom line.

Ask for the raise. Take a chance on either yourself, your skills, and your value. Be prepared to walk away from any opportunities that do not align. Explore other opportunities that do align not just with your values, but with your sense of worth.

Depending on where you are you should track your income, debt, credit score, investments, all while paying special attention to the numbers that directly impact where you are on your wealth journey.

Next, track your emotions about money. The actions you take with your money stem from the feelings you have. Remember, decisions are first made on an emotional level and then justified with logic. Every decision that you are making with your money starts either with how you are feeling or how you want to feel.

By tracking your emotional responses to money, finances, and wealth, you can identify triggers. What is the spark that sets off this specific chain reaction of actions? What happens just before you click the Amazon app to just "browse" but end up hitting "place order"? What happens at work or with your spouse that has you beating yourself up about the money you wish you had?

It is important to track your emotions from a third person perspective. You are simply observing what happened and how it felt. Don't fall into the trap of blaming or beating up yourself. That will not be helpful.

Tracking emotions also helps you identify patterns. That domino effect of actions that you feel helpless to stop. By the time these patterns are established they are operating from a subconscious level. So, breaking the pattern will be most successful if it can be stopped before it even begins. By identifying your triggers, you can better control and eliminate the undesirable actions that happen as a result.

The process of tracking your emotions is best accomplished in a journal format. Not everyone is keen to use pen and paper to record their thoughts. I like to store my entries as voice memos that I save to a secure, password protected folder. You may choose to write short form, bullet point entries. Whichever way you journal your emotions about money, do it consistently. You will glean a host of information from it when you look back and see what happened and when. Big indicators come out of you tracking your emotions.

I worked with Beth and her husband a few years ago. She admitted that she knew she shouldn't be spending as much as she did, but she couldn't seem to help herself. Now understand that this is a well-educated woman with an upper management position. She was no fool, but she couldn't shake this crazy spending.

We did an exercise to record and track how she was feeling when the crazy urge to spend came on and we uncovered a very eye-opening trigger.

Those seemingly uncontrollable spending binges happened whenever she felt she had to get back at someone or something. If she felt marginalized at work or felt hurt by her husband, she would head to the mall and swipe away the pain. We called it revenge spending. She would get back at all the people who hurt her by spending her way to her "happy place". The problem was that, in trying to get back at them she was causing herself financial pain and burying unresolved emotional pain.

By tracking her emotions we identified the root cause of her behaviour and then created healthier outlets for her pain. She had fun with exploring the possible installation of a boxing bag with a printout of her husband's face stuck onto it. Not sure if that ever happened but she started walking and got back to the gym regularly. She also planned to go back to her therapist for regular visits.

Her emotions had the answers, and she was able to devise a solution.

The final thing to track is the driving force behind your actions and decisions. When you build wealth, the ultimate outcomes you are seeking can be summarized as either choice, freedom, and impact.

At every age and every stage, you are looking for either of these outcomes and to varying degrees as your wealth journey progresses. Tracking how you make decisions will allow you to identify the driving factors that guide how you spend your money.

You will either make decisions based on your need for choices, your need for freedom, or your need for impact. What does that look like?

When choices are your most important priority you will be making decisions based on what you need versus what you want. This looks like you at the grocery store buying the toilet paper that's on sale as opposed to the one you really enjoy using. Or buying the general admission ticket for the professional development conference when you would have loved to have the VIP experience. That happens at the initial stages of the wealth journey. Your earning and spending decisions are predominantly guided by what you need. But as you grow and have success at that level, you find yourself starting to spend on things you want, not just what you need to get by.

Being driven by freedom, you will make decisions that compare price against personal value. It is no longer a 'needs versus wants' conversation. As you seek freedom you start paying attention to what has more value to you as opposed to what price you can afford. You choose to take a job that may pay less but has a better benefits package. You exercise the freedom to walk away from the appliance that is not in the colour you want. You can buy the car you want with the features you enjoy as opposed to settling to the one with a payment plan you can afford. Value begins driving your decisions and not cost.

Decisions will lastly be driven by what you want to experience versus the impact you want to have. At the highest levels of your growth in becoming wealthy on purpose, your decisions will move away from what you want and start moving towards how you want to impact others. Instead of leading your decision making with what's in it for you, you begin looking at how your decision would impact those people and causes that are important to you.

It could be a political issue or social enterprise. It could be our planet or the legacy you will leave to your grandchildren. Whatever it is you can now make it a priority because you likely already have everything you need or want for yourself.

Tracking how you make your money decisions will indicate growth in your relationship with money and where you should be focusing next. And any lack of progress would point to a need to revisit your clarity and alignment.

Tracking your wealth stats should be threefold – numbers, emotions, and decisions. Whatever you use to do your tracking - it must be something you can maintain, it is something with which you can connect.

Now, tracking without review is useless so set regular intervals when you will review all the areas that you are tracking. Compare them to the points where you want to be. Explain any shortfalls. Celebrate all goals met and exceeded. Track and review for wealth success.

JOURNAL PROMPTS

Where are you now on your wealth journey? What areas do you need to keep better track of? What tools can you use to help you with your tracking?

_____

_____

_____

_____

_____

_____

_____

_____

_____

_____

_____

_____

_____

WHY YOUR WEALTH RESULTS ARE INCONSISTENT

So, you've been tracking your wealth stats and you realize that you're on a rollercoaster. Today you feel good. You have money, spending is within your plan, and savings are on track. Tomorrow you are stressed out and anxious, binge spending and losing ground on your goals. It's like going from payday to broke in 10 seconds flat and repeating that experience over and over again.

Why does that happen? Why is it that your wealth experience is so inconsistent?

Your wealth experience does not have to be a rollercoaster. There will naturally be times when things don't go as planned. But being wealthy on purpose does not need to have those steep climbs to unsustainable peaks that result to crashing into deep, dark valleys of lack or anxiety.

I will share what I think are five reasons why your wealth might be inconsistent. Four of those reasons can be corrected and one, the final one, you should embrace.

Your foundation is unstable.

I see so many women trying to build empires when they still have a lack mentality and cannot string together a consistent cashflow track record. These women want to have wealthy people's experiences without doing the foundational work. The result? Winning the lottery and losing it all. Getting that raise at work and ending up in deeper debt than before. It's like watching your toddler trying to walk in your stilettos. No grace, no balance, no style. And, in quick time, without fail, an unwieldy tumble that may lead to tears and possible injury.

Instead, focus on building a strong mental, emotional, and financial foundation on which to build wealth. Nurture all aspects of your being so you can create a solid base on which to not just create wealth but to create wealth on purpose.

Create healthy habits that lead to beneficial actions you take with your money. Develop a healthy money mindset that fosters abundance and expansion and not lack and contraction. Keep an open mind to what is possible. That foundation will help you minimize the roller coaster and create sustainable wealth.

That foundation also provides a cushion for the challenging times that are sure to come along. You will weather financial storms far better if your foundation is solid. You can come through the challenges better and as a result bounce back that much faster. Healthy financial habits and thoughts together form a great foundation on which to create purposeful, consistent wealth.

Unsustainable expectations

Some of my best clients turn out to be their own worst enemies. They are super committed, not making any more excuses. They're ready to plow through anything that even thinks of getting in their way.

Those same clients are the ones that expect the debt that they may have accumulated over 5, 10, 15 years to disappear in a year. Not impossible but how sustainable is that for the long haul? How long before you are resentful of all you have to give up in order to make that happen? Not long at all and then everything falls apart and your progress stalls or, sometimes, you even start going backwards.

Those expectations set you up for failure because the solutions you employ are impractical.

Like a couple that I worked with. They were so determined to get into their first house that they wanted to cut all fast food. Understandably, they were shocked to discover that they were spending over $800 on convenience foods. So, they created their plan to cook all their meals at home, not eat out or order in. A great ideal. But can you imagine what it would take to go from spending $800+ a month on fast foods to $0? The result they wanted required behaviours to be adjusted, triggers identified, and habits changed. This is unrealistic in the time frame that they proposed.

I was able to guide them to a more sustainable approach to saving for their down payment. One that they could maintain while working on their habits. And there were still opportunities along the way to do some extra saving if they chose to.

Insufficient Income

We have been taught that we must cut and sacrifice our way to wealth. I guess that works for some. But it is very possible that your challenge is not in spending less. It is in earning more.

The days of getting a good job, working for 30 years, and retiring with the gold watch are no more. Not only are those days gone but they're not coming back. So, with employment being so precarious, you need multiple sources of income. These sources should also be sufficiently diverse so that if something were to happen on a sector-wide basis, you can cushion the blow with some other revenue sources.

If you are an employee, maximize your earnings. Ask for the raise and be compensated according to your worth. From that paycheque, create other streams of income from investments, real estate, a side hustle, and so on. As long as you love what you do, your money will be well positioned to multiply for you.

If you are a business owner, charge appropriately for your services. Create multiple offerings and automate your revenue generation systems. Hire and outsource your operations so that you can keep earning even while you're taking vacation. Pay yourself well!

A single, insufficient source of income won't last and will cause you to suffer the results of inconsistent wealth. So, explore the opportunities that exist for you to create income. Not income to just get by but income that will help you thrive and have the extraordinary experiences that you dream about. Wealth is all about having extraordinary outcomes.

Incompatible Strategies

Imagine you are great at technical analysis but have no time to commit to the research needed to get the results you want out of your investments. There are more important things that need your attention. Or maybe you hate having to make quick decisions but your neighbour swears by this day trading platform where he makes all this money day in and day out.

Both of these are examples of great strategies that just won't work for you because it goes against who you are on an innate level. They are incompatible with who and where you are.

The problem comes along when you try to force a fit. When you try to force compatibility. You sacrifice and turn yourself inside out for a method to fit and for things to go well. But when you finally realize that you cannot keep being who you're not or sacrificing those important things in your life, things start falling apart.

There are so many avenues to create wealth that there is absolutely no need to force a fit with incompatible strategies. Innovate and get creative.

The four reasons that I shared above for inconsistent wealth can be adjusted and corrected. This next contributor to inconsistent wealth results should be embraced.

'Tis the season

I am an immigrant to Canada, and I came from a country where there was only one season—heat! Well, we have a rainy season and a dry season, but the prevailing experience is heat. In coming to Canada, I got to experience a temperate climate. I could see firsthand, and not just in the movies, the amazing things that happen as seasons change. I saw trees that look dead come back to life with vibrant buds and full foliage. I experienced the intensity of winter cold and the vibrancy of summer heat. And through all this I noticed that there was a rhythm to it all. A rightness about each season as they followed each other.

With your journey to wealth, it is entirely possible that you have addressed all the other contributors to inconsistent results and still are having a hard time keeping the momentum or forward motion you want to see. In that case, consider that you may simply be in a season of your wealth journey where you must go inward. This might not be your time to be producing and increasing. It may be time to restore and review.

Every season is not about producing and multiplying. It is not always time to be spreading out. Sometimes you need to be planning, dreaming, exploring, and pouring into yourself. In that time, you get to catch your breath, take stock of how far you've come, and prepare yourself for the next stage. For that next big adventure with your finances.

You don't have to be concerned in that case because you are working your plan. Remember, you worked on your clarity and alignment. You have created an aligned strategy and are tracking and reviewing. With all those in place you can rest assured that this season you're in is temporary and much needed. Embrace it.

This approach will allow you to better manage any challenges that come your way in that season. You can sleep better and be less anxious. You can remain excited about your dreams being realized and stay focused on your purpose.

Stop fighting the seasons of wealth building.

Make peace with the shedding that is needed in order to make space for new opportunities. You may need to shed poor performing investments, liquidate assets, or let go of friendships that no longer lift you up. Embrace that.

Pace yourself through the big drain of your time and resources that come with the spring of your new ideas and renewed visions for wealth. It might take a lot out of you in the short term but lean into it. Spring is here.

Be invigorated by the heat of performance when you can see actual signs of growth. You can see the portfolios growing, the debts are being paid down nicely, and the cashflow plans allow you to have a life while saving and investing. Let that energize you.

Celebrate your harvest of positive results. All your hard work has paid off in your improved credit score, your growing real estate portfolio, your daughter's post-secondary education being fully funded. Use that celebration to prepare for the next dream to come true. For another goal to be realized.

Embrace all the seasons of your wealth. They are all necessary and a healthy part of your wealth journey.

I think the idea of trusting in the seasons of wealth is a great reminder that there is always the divine component to your life experience. Learn to trust that God's got you so you can let go. Trust the process of wealth creation.

Trust the process, do your part and rest in the power of your purpose. Embrace the season that you are in, knowing that everything you need will be there when you need it. In doing so your journey to wealth will be more purposeful, more fulfilling. And that is a recipe for a life well-lived.

JOURNAL PROMPTS

What is something you can work on that would help to get more consistent, positive financial results? Could this be a season of renewal for you? How would you know if it was?

_____

_____

_____

_____

_____

_____

_____

_____

_____

_____

_____

_____

_____

GUARANTEED
WEALTH - HERE'S HOW

In a world full of money-back guarantees it would be nice if we could get our money back when we make financial mistakes. For those "oopsies" spending moments and the "I hadn't thought of that" investment decisions. Unfortunately, the world does not work that way. Nothing is guaranteed, not even the best laid out strategy in the world can guarantee you specific results. I think, though, that you should do your very best to live your best life and make decisions that come as close as possible to guaranteeing your desired outcome.

Can you guarantee your wealth? If you can, how? How can you guarantee that the vision you took the time to seek out and refine will come to fruition? How can you eliminate the risk of loss, circumstance and time that could so easily mess up your dream?

Short answer – no you can't guarantee wealth. You can, however, set yourself up for success, in both the short and long term. You can position yourself as best as humanly possible to create the purpose driven life you desire and create the wealth needed to fund it. The answer lies in making use of a tension that is created along our journey to wealth.

This tension exists between the realities of your current situation and the power of the vision of your future. This tug and pull is happening because your present reality places us at quite a distance away from where you want to be. Yet your future vision is so compelling, so real to you, that you feel pulled in opposite directions. The key to setting yourself up for success is tapping into that tension. Don't try to eliminate it. Use it. Give it directionality and let it provide the fuel you need to get going and keep going on your road to wealth.

Too often that tension, when not properly channeled, deters you from the goal. It breaks you and pushes you away. That tension can cause you mental, relational, emotional pain because you have not yet learned how to harness it for your advantage. It makes the experience discouraging, overwhelming, and constricting.

What you want to do to help guarantee your wealth results is use that tension to create a force that is expansive and draws you to your vision. Hitch you present to your dream of the future and let your vision pull you forward.

But how do you do that? How do you maintain that healthy tension that makes your results almost effortless? Where you find yourself just naturally being drawn to the manifestation of wealth and purpose, freedom, and impact, and all that good stuff that I keep telling you about? Here's how you do it.

You must live a wealthy life every day. You must practice that wealthy state of mind every day. Here's a formula I discovered that aligns perfectly well with deliberately living a life of wealth on a daily basis.

First, visualize and affirm your vision every day, in fact, many times a day. I have reservations about how affirmations are being marketed as a magic wand for wealth, but they are beneficial when used in tandem with the other steps I will share here.

The challenge I see with affirmations is when you stand in the mirror and recite these mantras that are not authentic to you or your vision because you haven't yet done the work of clarity and alignment. You end up affirming things that you cannot claim, and to which you do not have a genuine connection.

Once you have done the inner work, you can create your own meaningful and aligned affirmations and practice them consistently to keep that vision purposeful and magnetic.

Secondly, if you want to guarantee your wealth results, you must plan and take action as if your result has already been accomplished. It sounds so simple but you may be stuck in either the planning or action stages.

Some of us love planning things out. We enjoy laying out how all the moving parts would come together. We enjoy thinking through possible contingencies and creating alternate strategies just in case. Yet we are challenged when it is time to move these plans from theory to practice.

For others, it is the opposite. We are anxiously awaiting the director's call for "Action!". Yet we can't be bothered to sit and plan out a thorough approach to wealth.

You being stuck might be a personality trait or a stress avoidance tactic. Either way, neither state is ideal. Whatever the reason is that you're stuck, get support in the areas where you need help. You may need a professional coach like me to help you create your best outcomes in the quickest time possible. You may call on your friends to keep you accountable. You may call on a community of support from likeminded women to cheer you on. Whatever you need, go get it.

One secret ingredient in the "doing" part of this step is to execute your plan as if you have already succeeded. Don't taint your wealth journey with worry, doubt, and self-deprecation. If you trust in the power of your purpose and hold fast to your vision, then you must also trust that your actions are the right ones. You have been inspired with the right moves for this stage in your journey.

Remember that part of your doing is for the purpose of learning and growing. Doing doesn't mean not failing. It means experiencing, sharing, and being part of the creation process.

Planning and doing creates momentum. The more you do the more you can reinforce the truth that you are doing the right things. You are creating the desired results.

The final step to guaranteeing your wealth results is one that is often overlooked. If you ignore this last step then you are guaranteeing burnout, discouragement, overwhelm, and lack which are the opposite of what you want to achieve.

The third step in living wealthy every day is to rest and review.

Review your plans, strategies, affirmations, and vision. Your review should follow a sequence – review, celebrate, and recalibrate.

I guarantee that when you stop to catch a breath, take a look at what is or isn't working, and celebrate everything, you will be better positioned to create the wealth you desire.

Celebrate the challenges you faced and the mistakes you made because you learned something through all of it. Guess what? The fact that you are sitting here in this moment, reading this book means that every single challenge you have faced up to this moment, you have come through it. You have been changed by it and grown through it. Celebrate that!

My personal trials, failures, and challenges with money led to the creation of this C|A|R|E methodology which has been so instrumental in helping women create wealth. How can I not celebrate my cheque-bouncing, professional financial hypocrite days that brought me to this? Every challenge that I faced has been part of me creating and living this blessed life now. I celebrate it all.

And let us not forget to celebrate our wins too! Celebrate the decision you made that turned out to be the best decision. Celebrate the successful course you invested in and actually completed. Throw yourself a party to mark that milestone birthday. Take that vacation or spa weekend to reward yourself for sticking to your cashflow plan and loving every minute of it.

So, while there are no guarantees in money, you can set yourself up for success by living in a wealthy mindset daily.

Visualize and affirm your vision.

Plan and take action.

Rest and review.

Live the wealthy life every day, and even though there's tension between where you are now with your money and where your vision is trying to get you to, harness that tension and channel it so your vision pulls you to itself. Trust that the vision that you have been given is for you. It is already done.

JOURNAL PROMPTS

What can you do to help affirm your vision of the future daily? Do you think you are naturally a planner or an action taker? How can you generate some momentum in your wealth journey?

EVOLUTION

THE EVOLUTION OF
YOUR WEALTH JOURNEY

The idea of evolution on its own can be a polarizing topic between evolutionists and creationists. I'll invite you to step away from that debate as we explore the application of evolution in the world of personal finance.

As a woman creating wealth on purpose, you are driven, and, at this point, you know what you are all about. You have achieved clarity and alignment in your wealth journey and are getting the results you worked diligently to achieve. Things are working out. So what's next for you? It is time for you and your journey to evolve.

There's this thing that happens once you reach a goal. You realize that there is another level that now has become visible. Another goal you can be aiming for. There is another level of freedom, experience, and impact, that you can aspire to reach.

I think that this is the beautiful thing about your wealth journey. As you grow and achieve, new and exciting opportunities open up to you. The journey is never boring.

Let's explore why I choose to use the word evolution, as opposed to adaptation, to describe the next step in your journey to wealth. I was deliberate in using evolution at this stage not because of the dictionary meaning.

Both adaptation and evolution speak of a change that is occurring. So, they can both be used in wealth to convey the idea of changing and becoming. These changes could be in your life situation, your lifestyle, and your friendships. All of these can and will change. Here is the nuance that for me differentiates adaptation from evolution.

In my mind, adaptation in wealth has to do with changing in order to stay or to remain. Evolution in wealth speaks of changing to thrive.

I think of adaptation similarly to ideas like tolerance. I mean, who wants to be tolerated. We want to be loved, celebrated, appreciated. Similarly, why should I adapt to less-than-ideal circumstances. Why should I adapt to what is around me to maintain the status quo?

I much prefer the idea of evolving. Of making fundamental changes that enable me and the environment around me to thrive. That is a big deal!

You are not living this life to be tolerated. You want to be embraced, loved, welcomed with open arms, and celebrated. And I think the same thing when it comes to wealth.

There is that unspoken connotation in the word adapt that kind of speaks to accepting less than. Accepting where you are at and just making do. And in that sense, adapting should not be used in the same sentence as wealth. As a woman on your journey to wealth, becoming your best and highest self as your wealth is increasing and as you are moving on to new and amazing adventures and experiences: That is evolving.

146

The evolution of your wealth is just the beginning because when you become a wealthy woman on purpose, I mean the sky is the limit.

JOURNAL PROMPTS

Have you been adapting and making do in your current financial circumstances? What have you missed out on because you decided to adapt rather than evolve? Role play a scenario where you have evolved into your wealthy, purposeful self.

THE ELUSIVE FINISH LINE

We are constantly evolving. Constantly changing as we have new experiences with money, relationships, and ourselves. This reality flies contrary to the idea of a finish line in wealth.

This supposed finish line would be where you'd say, "Now that I have $X in my account I am wealthy. I no longer need to do mindset work or develop and review new strategies. I have made it!"

Well, I hate to break it to you but that notion is an illusion. The finish line that you are looking for is more of a journey marker. A rest stop. A check point where you can catch your breath to start again.

Mistaking the rest stop for a finish line is very defeating. It makes you feel like you are failing. As if someone is always moving the goalpost. You get so tired as a result because you are not able to properly pace yourself. Wealth is more about what's happening in your head than what you are accumulating.

Do you ever tell yourself, "Once I reach this age I will be done learning and growing"? I doubt it. As long as you live you will keep learning and growing and it is the same with wealth. Wealth is a state of being, so as long as you live you will be on a wealth journey.

Let go of the illusion of a finish line because it will either defeat you or cause you to burn out. The idea of a finish line being so far away could even cause you to not start at all.

Instead of nurturing the idea of a finish line, think of how you can most enjoy this journey.

I love driving and consider myself a very good driver. I hate road trips. It's not the driving part I hate so much as the length of drives. It takes too long! I just want to get there already!

For years, we would make the trek to New York by car. From where I live in Canada, the drive to our destination was roughly eight hours. When our daughters were babies, we would drive through the night. We would start out at around their normal bedtime. Cozy them up in their pajamas with blankets and pillows in the back. They still talk about the blanket forts they would build in the back as we drove. They loved it. Eventually, they would fall asleep, and my husband and I would alternate driving and resting. It worked beautifully for the kids…no restlessness or incessant "are we there yet's".

I hated every minute of being on the road. I hated having to stay alert when I wanted to sleep. I hated having to watch the kilometers click over ever so slowly. I hated the journey to get there but I loved arriving. I loved meeting with my family and getting up to all our shenanigans. I loved the destination but not the process of getting to it. That made for a mixed bag of emotions that tainted the whole experience.

I knew something had to change because I was not about to give up on connecting with my family anytime soon. I had to figure out a way that I could enjoy the journey. So, we made some adjustments.

We no longer travel through the night. We drive in the daytime, at a time when our bodies would naturally be alert and active. We also no longer just put the pedal to the metal to get there. Instead, we decided to take out time, enjoy the sites, take in a stop here and there. Essentially, we decided to just enjoy the journey. The lines at the border didn't bother us and random detours were okay too. It became a much more enjoyable experience when I found joy in both the journey and the destination.

It is the same thing for you as a woman creating the life you desire and deserve. Instead of sacrificing and creating massive discomfort and upheaval in your life for the illusion of reaching a finish line, choose to enjoy the process of becoming that wealthy woman on purpose. Immerse yourself in every step you take along the way.

One of the contributing events to my becoming a wealth coach happened while I was still in traditional advisory practice. This couple came in. The husband was retiring with a very robust pension package and they were excited.

They were looking forward to enjoying their retirement. They had sacrificed much through their working years so that they could get to this time. And they were finally ready to live it up. They were ready to travel, renovate the house, repair the cottage. They were ready to splurge a little, live a little. The whole shebang. Plan in place, they were off. A few months later they came back into the office. They asked us to help rejig things a bit because they had found out that he had a brain tumor.

At the time, I remember thinking that they did it right so why is this happening to them. They worked, sacrificed, did without. They saved and delayed gratification while they were young and strong. They invested in their children and set them up well. They did all the right things and now this. Why? It wasn't right. They'd given up so much along the journey to retirement only to have fate change the rules, move the goal post on them just as they arrived.

Through that experience it became so painfully clear to me that you cannot live life waiting for some magic moment to have the experiences you value. There is no guarantee that you will make it to this elusive moment in time. You may not live to retirement. Or your health may fail along the way. Enjoy your wealth today. You deserve a life experience that is full and rich today!

Think of one thing you could do in the next month or two that can bring joy and fulfilment to your life. Something that you can use your money to do that will create a beautiful memory. It doesn't have to cost much. It could be something as simple as going out and having an ice cream cone while walking along the beach reminiscing with friends or having some much needed me time. Use your money to find joy in the present.

If you work this process correctly, you will naturally release the illusion of the finish line because you will remember every day that you are wealthy now, in this very moment.

Your journey will also be more enjoyable if you can find the right companions to go with you. That may mean opening yourself to new friendships and ending those that no longer uplift you.

Your spouse might not be the best person to partner with on this journey. That does not mean you have to separate. It just means that when it comes to wealth building, you will be fueled and supported by someone else.

If you had to deal with lots of generational money trauma, then your parents or siblings might also not be a good fit for your support system unless they actively work on healing themselves.

It's okay. Find your wealth journey mate wherever he or she may happen to be. Look for someone who has the same mindset as you and whose strength might not be yours. Someone whom you can help and who can help you. The important thing is to make sure that you are on the same page in your approach to wealth. That you are both committed to becoming wealthy on purpose.

JOURNAL PROMPTS

Is there any area of your financial life where you may have given up because your goal seemed too far out of reach? Where can you rethink your idea of "arriving" in wealth? Who could you identify as a great wealth journey mate?

_____

_____

_____

_____

_____

_____

_____

_____

_____

_____

_____

_____

_____

CONTENTMENT AND HUNGER
– THE HAPPY MEDIUM

If you go back a few chapters, we explored the tension that exists between where you are now and where you want to get to. Between your present reality and your future vision. I encouraged you to harness that tension and use it to pull you to your vision.

The mechanics of that process lie in being content in your present while remaining hungry for the future. There is a way to be content, whole, and complete in our current situation even as we actively drive towards our vision and purpose.

Here are three things that will help you nurture contentment in your current financial circumstances.

Live every day in gratitude.

Gratitude exists outside of your financial circumstances. So, whatever those circumstances happen to be you can still live in gratitude. You might be underpaid, perhaps underemployed. There may be some bills that you need to be creatively spreading your money across instead of paying them all off like you want to. You want to be investing but you're not there yet. You might even be a little scared about your current situation.

All of these can be true, but gratitude exists outside of these situations.

In fact, gratitude is about being. It is about celebrating the gift that is life. Gratitude begins from the inside and emanates out. You can be grateful in all circumstances because our gratitude colours all your circumstances with light.

Whether you are having a tough time or not, stressed out or not, gratitude coming from the inside puts a different spin on things.

True gratitude for your finances does not come from your financial situation. It comes from inside you and spills over onto your financial situation. So, if your finances are fantastic, you are grateful. If your finances are a mess, still grateful.

Accept that your current financial circumstances are the building blocks of your vision.

They are part of that jigsaw puzzle that is being put together to create your vision and bring it to life. Why not embrace them?

I didn't say go on and keep spending like there is no tomorrow. Don't keep maxing out your credit cards. No, that's not what I mean.

What I mean is every experience that you are having right now, everything that you have won, everything that you have lost, every situation that has either challenged or affirmed you is part of who you are becoming and thus, part of that vision that you are hungry for.

Do not run away from it. Instead make it part of that healthy balance that you are existing with. Make it part of your life of contentment where you have forgiven yourself for your mistakes. Part of your life where you look back and say never again and feed that hunger for better.

Acknowledge that you are not defined by your financial circumstances.

Who you are is not determined by your current financial state. When you wrap your head around this thought you can release yourself to have your unique experience with wealth.

Wouldn't it be amazing if you released yourself from being defined by your money? You are not your money. You are not your credit card bill. You are not your paycheck. You are not your credit score.

Now, it is no longer a question of you being or becoming anything that someone else thinks you should be. You get to be you with gratitude, with the definition of yourself that comes from the inside out, and with an appreciation that it is all part of the big picture. The happy days, the challenging days, the ups and the downs, the ins and the outs, the various seasons of wealth. All are part of the experience in building wealth.

Now that you have nurtured contentment with your present situation, how do you stay hungry? How do you maintain the drive needed to achieve your goals and dreams?

This might sound counterintuitive but the more content you are in your current situation the easier it will be for you to work towards your dreams.

Your contentment takes the pain out of your present situation. Sure, it is less than ideal but you have discovered ways to thrive within it. That creates an atmosphere where amazing things happen effortlessly because you are no longer in a dark and painful place. The pain of blame, self-loathing, disappointment, and loss have been neutralized.

Your pain has been replaced with vision and hope, joy, and gratitude. In such an environment, your hunger is tempered with grace, and you can look forward to the evolution of your finances without desperation.

Your hunger for the future is no longer all-consuming because you are not starving for wealth. You are experiencing wealth every day. The hunger you feel is simply the excitement of anticipating what's next for you.

JOURNAL PROMPTS

Have you been consumed with a financial goal to the detriment of your relationship, health, or something else? Do you feel desperate to make things happen with your money? What daily gratitude practice can you start doing?

_____

_____

_____

_____

_____

_____

_____

_____

_____

_____

_____

_____

_____

_____

BREAKING
THE DREAM CEILING

Every year I do a review of my accomplishments. I look at the goals I hit, the ones I missed, and the ones that no longer excite me. Then I create new goals for the next 1, 3, 5 and 10 years.

One year as I was doing this exercise, I was able to celebrate some dreams being realized so a few items got checked off the list. Other goals were moved closer in time, so instead of it happening in the next 5 years, I was able to move some down to 3 years. Great progress was being made.

I ran into a problem, however, when I got to the 10-year goals. I had nothing. I drew a complete blank. I couldn't think of anything that I wanted to accomplish in the next 10 years. I felt as though everything that I wanted to accomplish would get done in the next 1, 3, or 5 years. I was shaken. How can that be?

There is still so much life to live, experiences to have, and money to be made. I didn't see my purpose ending after 5 years. That was not in the vision. All the same it would appear that I had run out of wealth goals.

Has that ever happened to you? Have you experienced a time when you just did not know what the next thing was supposed to be? Have you ever had the experience where you are intentional with your gratitude, and you tap into your purpose consistently but are not sure what your goals should be?

As you evolve in your wealth journey you might have that experience so I'll share with you how you can break the dream ceiling.

This dream ceiling might come from self-imposed limitations on a subconscious level that you put in place to keep you safe. Other limitations on your dreams can come from external sources to "keep you in your place". Regardless of the source, it is to your benefit to break the dream ceiling. There is more out there for you and you owe it to yourself to break through.

First, go within and ask for direction. Cut away the noise around you. Pray, or meditate and seek guidance. When the answers you seek are not showing up in the physical world you need divine inspiration. It makes no sense to stay in a lost, unfulfilled state when you can access guidance from another source.

You see, it's not that there isn't another dream to be realized. It is instead a case where the vision is blurred or obscured. You need help to clear things off and remove the blocks. The dream is there but you need help to see it.

Next, expose yourself to big dreamers. They may not be naturally occurring where you are now. Your immediate circle of influence might be depending on you to create dreams for them. Or they might be content to remain where they are. They are not a source of inspiration for you.

In my case the examples of impactful wealth that I have seen still seemed to be outside of my realm of possibility. I remember my mentor saying to me, "You do not know what to dream for because you have not seen it in your life or around you."

I want to have epic impact. I want to touch the world like Sir Richard Branson is doing. I want to move the needle in big ways, but based on where I am sitting right now, I don't yet see how I can do it.

I couldn't discern a path to the dream and as a result I was blocking the dream entirely.

Set the intention to meet people who have dreams that are different from yours. People who are achieving freedom and impact that you hadn't even thought possible.

Attend the keynote presentation of the woman who started a capital lending fund from scratch for women owned businesses. Invite the CEO of that innovative startup to lunch. Connect with that real estate investor who is building housing specifically for marginalized communities.

Who is dreaming different, bigger dreams than you? Go find them and become part of their circle.

Finally, recalibrate for clarity and alignment. Now that you have been inspired, recommit yourself to seeking and finding clarity and alignment for the way forward. Do not take the next steps forward until you have found that.

Consider what options now lay before you and devise your plan to fit your purpose. Recalibrate your results so you know what you will be measuring for this leg of the journey and set your plan in motion.

You are becoming a wealthy woman on purpose so there will always be another level or stage to be reaching for. Never question if there is another dream ahead. There is. You only need to see clearly and find the inspiration to take action.

JOURNAL PROMPTS

Who is someone you'd like to meet who is doing what you'd like to be doing with your money? How could you meet them or get to know them better? When can you schedule some quiet time to seek direction or next steps for your wealth journey?

_____

_____

_____

_____

_____

_____

_____

_____

_____

_____

_____

_____

_____

YOU - A WEALTHY WOMAN ON PURPOSE

I am excited about what becoming a wealthy woman on purpose could mean for you, your family, and community. The results of this journey are infinite. You may not even realize the impact this journey will have, who you can inspire and whose life you can change.

I hope that you have been inspired, empowered, and equipped through this guide. You are on a life journey. One to be enjoyed, to be challenged, and to be fulfilled by. You will keep learning and growing. You will keep becoming.

While the specifics of your journey may be unique to you, you are now part of a global movement of women, focused on creating wealth and using it purposefully.

The previous chapters have provided you with insights that are bold and revolutionary in the personal finance space. You have been shown how to lead your wealth journey with heart, not numbers. You have seen how clarity and alignment are the place to start on your journey to wealth. And that wealth infused with purpose is the ultimate life experience.

My final advice to you.

1. Be confident. Take bold action. You will ruffle feathers as you deploy your plan. You will rock the boat as you find your footing. People will say that you've changed. That's okay. You haven't so much changed as you've evolved. You are still the same wonderful human you have always been. Now you've simply chosen to create an extraordinary life that is worth living.

2. Be unapologetic: Don't apologize for being committed to your goal. Don't apologize for realizing extraordinary results. Don't apologize for your ability to have epic experiences. And don't use your wealth in the mistaken attempt to buy others' acceptance. Your true supporters will celebrate your successes and not resent you for them.

3. Be You. The world needs you and your special, unique purpose. The world is waiting for you to get on this wealth journey and create the changes you have been gifted to address. You and your wealth are a gift to your world.

I celebrate you as that wealthy woman. I celebrate what you have achieved and will create. The way you have embraced your present while working towards your future. I celebrate your influence and impact and the courage you have developed to live the life you desire and deserve.

So, how are you celebrating? I challenge you right now to plan your celebration. Whatever that looks like for you, celebrate this moment in your journey. Celebrate you.

This moment in time will be your springboard to the next place level of wealth. And you get to do it your way. Regardless of your unique combination of strategies, don't just dream it or plan it. Do it.

You have this opportunity to experience luxurious stability. Don't run away from extraordinary and settle for a boring, humdrum, lackluster life. You were not created for boring. Mediocrity was never part of the plan for you. You were created for the purposeful extraordinary. Becoming a wealthy woman on purpose provides that opportunity.

ACKNOWLEDGEMENTS

I have to thank my daughters for being my biggest cheerleaders. You girls, pardon me, ladies have supported me along this journey in ways that I could never have imagined. You both are the best thing I have produced in this world and you make me proud every single day. Thanks for choosing me to be your mom.

None of this would be possible without my parents who sacrificed for me in ways that I could never repay. Thank you for being exactly who I needed you to be in order for me to become who I am today. It is on your shoulders that I stand today, sharing what you have taught me with the world.

To my husband, thank you for helping me to grow into my best, bravest self. Every day you give me reasons to keep pressing on toward my dreams.

To my coaches Claudine Pereira and Shelagh Cummins. What can I say? You gave me the tools I needed to take me from an entrepreneur to a CEO, and with that you provided the confidence to know that I was changing women's lives with my work. Thank you for believing in me and telling me what I needed to hear. You ladies are amazing!

To my mastermind queens Dee Boswell-Buck and Christen N James. You ladies heard it all! The ups, downs, and in betweens. Thank you for holding space for me and cheering me on through it all. Thanks for never letting me quit!

To publishing coach extraordinaire Uchechi Ezurike-Bosse and your awesome team that kept this project moving and me calm. You set my expectations and did not disappoint. Here's to our next project together.

My editor Danielle Hines for providing some much-needed affirmation that I had something worth writing and that the world would be blessed to read it.

And to every woman who has trusted me to guide her along the path to confident money management - Thank you.

ABOUT THE AUTHOR

Hadriana Leo is a Wealth Strategist, Coach, and Consultant. She is on a mission to inspire, empower, and equip women to unapologetically create wealth. Her unique methodology connects the head and heart so women can confidently walk their path to lasting wealth and legacy!

She worked successfully within the personal finance sector as a licensed representative offering investment and insurance services to her clients. After studying the behavioural components of money management, Hadriana launched her coaching practice in 2015.

Hadriana was born on the sunny island of St. Lucia and now lives just outside Toronto, Canada with her husband, two daughters, and golden doodle. She has a beautiful soprano voice, a big heart, and a dazzling smile. She enjoys using all her gifts to inspire.